# I want to be a chef
# BAKING

# I want to be a chef
# BAKING

MURDOCH BOOKS

# contents

# let's bake...

It's fun to cook baked goods such as sausage rolls, sweet and savoury muffins, pizzas, pies, cupcakes and cookies...and even more fun to eat them. Making them involves many techniques, such as whisking egg whites for meringues, icing cakes and rolling out pastry. With this book to help you, you'll soon be baking just like a professional chef.

## How to start

To be a successful cook, you must be organised. To produce the best results, a professional chef relies on a well-run, clean and tidy kitchen, and you should, too. There are some other important things you need to know to make cooking...and most particularly baking...a real pleasure.

◆ First, read all the way through the recipe and check the list of ingredients to make sure you have everything you need before you start. Having to run to the shops in the middle of making a cake is not a good idea.

◆ Have the right equipment close to hand. Put the kitchen scales out on the bench. Have wooden spoons and knives set out in a row.

◆ Prepare any baking tins or moulds. They may have to be greased with oil or butter, or lined with baking paper.

◆ Before you start cooking, set out all the ingredients that you will need on the kitchen bench. Open tins, peel and chop fruit and vegetables, grate cheese and measure flour, sugar and butter. Otherwise, you will have to stop and start all the time, which can be time consuming. And, it can create lots of mess. Be sure to clean up as you go.

◆ Read the recipe as you go and check that you're adding the ingredients in the right order.

◆ Preheat the oven when the recipe tells you to. See more information about oven use on the next page.

◆ Be sure to have a kitchen timer with an alarm function or have a clock handy, to keep track of cooking times. It's easy to forget when you put something in the oven and baked items can quickly spoil if left there too long.

## How to weigh and measure

It is very important that you measure ingredients carefully. The proportion of butter to flour, sugar to butter and so on is very precise in baking and the end result can be badly affected if you don't follow the recipe.

You'll see that three different scales for measuring are given in the recipes in this book: there are metric, imperial and cup measures. So, there should be something to suit every kitchen. A cup measure is a standard 250 ml (9 fl oz). Whichever scale you use, stay with it throughout a recipe and don't chop and change. If you like to measure in cups, stay with cup i. If you prefer to weigh things in grams, use only grams.

You will need:

◆ a set of dry measuring cups, usually in a set of four: a 250 ml (9 fl oz/1 cup) measure and 125 ml (4 fl oz/½ cup), 80 ml (2½ fl oz/⅓ cup) and 60 ml (2 fl oz/¼ cup) measures. These are used for ingredients such as flour and sugar.

◆ a liquid measuring cup with a lip. This should have lines on the side that clearly show the measures.

◆ a set of measuring spoons: 1 tablespoon, 1 teaspoon, ½ teaspoon and ¼ teaspoon. You can buy metal or plastic ones.

Liquid measures
Place the liquid measuring cup on the bench, then add some of the liquid and bend down so your eyes are level with the measurement marks. Check if you have too much or too little liquid and add or remove, as necessary.

Dry measures
Spoon dry ingredients into the measuring cup or spoon and then level them off with a knife or metal spatula. Cup and spoon measures for dry ingredients should be level, not heaped (unless the recipe specifically says otherwise).

## Special equipment

Baking tins for cake making come in all sorts of different shapes and sizes and it's a good idea to have a range of them to add variety. Some recipes need you to use a particular shape. For example, the little cakes known as friands use tins which are oval with straight sides. You'll also see ones that are shaped like a gold ingot with sloping sides, which can be used for the same purpose. Muffin tins with a different number of holes (4, 9 or 12) of

different sizes are handy, too. Mini bundt tins (round, fluted and with a hole in the middle) produce a very attractive result. An electric whisk is a big help for beating butter and sugar together until light and fluffy and for beating eggs into a cake mixture. It will also take the hard work out of making meringues, when you need to beat egg whites until they are stiff.

## Baking tips

You'll need to use special techniques and ways of working when making cakes and cookies. Here's what to do.

◆ As usual, first read the recipe. Take any chilled ingredients such as butter and eggs from the fridge and set aside on the kitchen bench to reach room temperature. If you need to beat butter and sugar together, you won't be able to work with the butter if it's in a hard, solid lump.

◆ Line tin(s) with baking paper, following the recipe instructions, or butter and dust lightly with flour. Use the shape and size of tin the recipe says, because this affects the cooking time.

◆ Before you turn on the oven, position the shelf in the centre of the oven and make sure there is enough room above it for the cake to rise. Preheat the oven to the temperature stated in the recipe.

◆ Weigh and measure all the ingredients properly before you start.

◆ Add eggs or egg yolks to a cake mixture one at a time, beating well after you add each one. Don't put all the eggs in together.

◆ To whisk egg whites, make sure both the bowl and the beaters (or whisk) are clean and dry. Just a hint of grease, and the egg whites won't whisk properly.

◆ Dry ingredients should be folded into a whisked egg and sugar mixture with a large metal spoon. Fold gently from the centre of the bowl outwards. Fold whisked egg whites into the other ingredients (not the other way round).

◆ Spoon thick cake batters into the prepared tin and pour in thinner batters. Smooth the surface of the batter with a spatula or the back of a spoon so that it is level and will cook and brown evenly.

## How to use the oven

If you're using the oven, place the shelves at the correct height before you turn it on. Always preheat the oven to the temperature given in the recipe before putting things in to cook. Most ovens have a light to show when the right temperature has been reached and you can put the food in.

If you have a fan-forced oven (ask an adult, if you're not sure), then the temperature will be a bit hotter than a normal oven. The temperatures given in the recipes in this book are for a normal oven. If you use a fan-forced oven, you don't need to worry about preheating it, but you will need to reduce the temperature for each recipe by about 10°C (18°F). This is most important for baking cakes, slices and cookies and other sweet things. It is less important for things such as roasts.

## Presentation

If you watch cooking programs on the television, you'll know that professional chefs always arrange food on the plate in an attractive way. They decorate desserts and cakes with such things as chocolate curls and swirls of cream. While you don't need to spend a lot of time doing this, it does add to the pleasure of eating if the food is arranged neatly and not just plopped on in a messy way. After all the trouble you've taken to cook something well, it makes sense to 'plate' it properly. Set the table with pretty china and colourful napkins.

## Food safety

Knowing how to store and transport food safely is very important. Spoiled food can make you ill. While there is less to worry about with baked goods such as cakes, it is important to know how to handle raw products such as meat and chicken, which you may use in a pie or some other baked dish.

How to handle uncooked meat
◆ As a general rule, raw meat will keep for up to 3 days in the fridge and up to 6 months in the freezer.

◆ To freeze meat, wrap each piece in plastic wrap, then put it in a freezer

### Food allergies

Some people have an allergy to a particular food and may become very ill if they eat it. If you're having friends round for something to eat, ask an adult in the family to find out if any of them has a food intolerance, so you don't include an ingredient it is dangerous for them to eat. If someone has a severe nut allergy (to peanuts, for example), make sure there are no foods containing even the tiniest amount. Don't serve nuts or small sweets to children under five; they could choke on them.

bag. Make sure that you get all the air out of the bag. Ask an adult if you need help. Label and date the bag because, once something is frozen, it is virtually impossible to recognise what it is.

◆ To thaw, put the meat on a large plate and leave it in the fridge. Allow enough time for it to defrost fully before starting to cook. If you're not sure, ask an adult. Depending on just how big the item is, it can take several hours or may need to be left overnight. Never thaw meat at room temperature or under water. Don't re-freeze thawed meat unless you have cooked it first.

How to handle uncooked chicken
Chicken should be treated very carefully as it can harbour dangerous bacteria.

◆ Keep it in the fridge for 2 days at the most, and up to 6 months in the freezer.

◆ Thaw chicken in the same way as meat. Cook it within 12 hours of thawing. Never let raw chicken (or other raw meat) come in contact with other foods in the fridge.

How to handle cooked food
◆ Cool hot food quickly that you need to store. Put it in the fridge as soon as steam has stopped rising.

◆ If you're packing food in a lunchbox, use one that's insulated or add a freezer pack. Don't pack hot foods in your lunchbox. First let them cool in the fridge overnight.

## Hygiene and personal safety

1  Always ask an adult for permission before you start to cook. And always ask for help if you are not confident with chopping or handling hot cake tins.

Remove toothpicks from food before serving to children under five.

2  Before you start, wash your hands well with soap and water, tie back long hair and wear an apron to protect your clothes. Have clean, dry oven gloves and tea towels handy.

3  When cooking on the stovetop, turn pan handles to the side so there's no danger of knocking them. When you are stirring, hold the pan handle firmly.

4  Never use electrical appliances near water. Always dry your hands carefully before you touch any appliance. When you have finished with it, switch it off at the power point and remove the plug from the wall before cleaning it.

5  Always use thick, dry oven gloves when getting things out of the oven.

6  Turn off the oven, hotplate or gas ring when you have finished using it.

## How to use this book
All the recipes are broken down into a few simple steps. They all have photographs so you can see what your finished product is going to look like. Some of the recipes have step-by-step photographs to help you with any techniques you may not know or are finding difficult to do.

And, finally...have fun cooking and enjoy your journey to becoming a top-notch chef.

# savoury bites

# mini scones with ham and cheese

## MAKES ABOUT 40

250 g (9 oz/2 cups) plain (all-purpose) flour

3 teaspoons baking powder

110 g (3¾ oz) butter

100 g (3½ oz) stilton cheese

2 tablespoons snipped chives

185 ml (6 fl oz/¾ cup) milk

### filling

4 tablespoons dijon mustard

150 g (5½ oz) shaved ham

100 g (3½ oz) cheddar cheese

1 Sift the flour, baking powder and ¾ teaspoon salt into a bowl. Grate the butter and cheese into the flour and rub in using your fingertips. Stir in the chives. Pour in the milk and combine with a fork until large clumps form. Turn onto a floured surface and press into a ball.

2 Preheat the oven to 220°C (425°F/Gas 7). Roll the dough out on a floured surface into a 15 x 25 cm (6 x 10 inch) rectangle. With the long edge of the dough facing you, fold in both ends so they meet in the centre, then fold the dough in half widthways. Roll again into a 15 x 25 cm (6 x 10 inch) rectangle, about 1 cm (½ inch) thick.

3 Cut rounds close together with a 3 cm (1¼ inch) cutter. Push the scraps together and roll and cut as before. Place 2.5 cm (1 inch) apart on a baking tray and refrigerate for 20 minutes. Bake for 10–12 minutes.

4 Cut the scones in half. Spread the bases with the mustard. Put a folded piece of ham on each bottom half, top with cheese, then replace the tops.

# tomato, bocconcini and basil muffins

### MAKES 24

170 g (6 oz) self-raising flour

½ teaspoon baking powder

185 ml (6 fl oz/¾ cup) milk

1 egg, beaten

1 roma (plum) tomato, chopped

2 bocconcini (fresh baby mozzarella cheese), chopped

1½ tablespoons shredded basil

30 g (1 oz) unsalted butter, melted and cooled

1 Preheat the oven to 200°C (400°F/Gas 6). Lightly grease 24 mini muffin holes.

2 Sift the flour and baking powder into a large bowl. Make a well in the centre.

3 Whisk the milk and eggs together, then pour into the well. Add the tomato, bocconcini, basil and melted butter. Fold gently until just combined—the mixture should be lumpy.

4 Divide the mixture evenly among the muffin holes. Bake for 25 minutes, or until golden. Cool for 5 minutes, then turn out onto a wire rack.

# parmesan, pumpkin and zucchini muffins

**MAKES 30**

100 g (3½ oz) pumpkin (winter squash),
peeled and roughly chopped

125 g (4½ oz/1 cup) self-raising flour

¼ teaspoon baking powder

35 g (1¼ oz) grated parmesan cheese

½ zucchini (courgette), grated

60 g (2¼ oz) unsalted butter, melted and
cooled

1 egg

100 ml (3½ oz) milk

½ tablespoon sesame seeds

2 tablespoons grated parmesan cheese,
extra

1 Preheat the oven to 190°C (375°F/
Gas 5). Line 30 mini muffin holes with
paper cases. Steam the pumpkin for
10 minutes. Mash until smooth.

2 Sift the flour and baking powder into
a bowl, then mix in the parmesan.
Make a well in the centre.

3 Put the pumpkin, zucchini and butter
in a separate bowl. Beat the egg.
Combine half of the beaten egg and
the milk and add to the pumpkin
mixture. Mix.

4 Add to the dry ingredients. Fold
in gently.

5 Divide the mixture evenly among
the muffin holes. Sprinkle with the
sesame seeds and extra parmesan.

6 Bake for 35 minutes, or until golden.
Cool for 5 minutes, then turn out onto
a wire rack.

# beef and tomato tarts

## MAKES 24

6 ready-rolled shortcrust (pie) pastry sheets

1 tablespoon oil

1 onion, chopped

2 garlic cloves, crushed

500 g (1 lb 2 oz) minced (ground) beef

2 tablespoons plain (all-purpose) flour

375 ml (13 fl oz/1½ cups) beef stock

4 tablespoons tomato sauce (ketchup)

2 teaspoons worcestershire sauce

½ teaspoon dried mixed herbs

2 small tomatoes, cut in half and sliced

½ teaspoon dried oregano leaves

extra tomato sauce (ketchup), to serve

1 Preheat the oven to 200°C (400°F/Gas 6).

2 Cut the pastry into 24 circles using a 7 cm (2¾ inch) round cutter. Press the circles into two lightly greased 12-hole patty pans or mini muffin tins.

3 Heat the oil in a heavy-based saucepan, add the onion and garlic and cook over medium heat for 2 minutes, or until the onion is soft. Add the beef and stir over high heat for 3 minutes, or until well browned and all the liquid has evaporated.

4 Add the flour, stir until combined, then cook over medium heat for 1 minute. Add the stock, sauces and herbs and stir over low heat until boiling. Reduce the heat to low and simmer for 5 minutes until reduced and thickened, stirring occasionally. Allow to cool.

5 Divide the filling among the pastry circles. Top each with two half slices of tomato and sprinkle with oregano. Bake for 25 minutes, or until the pastry is golden brown and crisp. Cover with tomato sauce and serve hot.

# sailors' knots

**MAKES ABOUT 24**

1 sheet ready-rolled puff pastry

1 egg, beaten

20 g (¾ oz) grated cheddar cheese

1 tablespoon sesame seeds

1 Preheat the oven to 210°C (415°F/Gas 6–7). Brush a baking tray with oil

2 Cut the pastry sheet in half, then across the width into 2 cm (¾ inch) strips.

3 Tie each of the strips into simple knots. Place onto the baking tray.

4 Brush the pastry lightly with beaten egg and sprinkle with the cheese and sesame seeds.

5 Bake for 10 minutes, or until puffed and golden. Cool on a wire rack

**Note:** These can be prepared up to 3 days in advance. Store in an airtight container in a cool, dry place.

# corn and red capsicum tartlets

## MAKES ABOUT 36

3 frozen puff pastry sheets, thawed

310 g (11 oz) tinned corn kernels, drained

150 g (5½ oz) red leicester cheese, grated

1 small red capsicum (pepper), finely chopped

2 eggs, lightly beaten

3 tablespoons buttermilk

170 ml (5½ fl oz/²/₃ cup) thick (double/heavy) cream

1 teaspoon dijon mustard

dash Tabasco sauce

1 Preheat the oven to 200°C (400°F/Gas 6). Lightly grease three 12-hole round-based patty pans or mini muffin tins. Using a 6 cm (2½ inch) round pastry cutter, cut circles from the pastry sheets. Press the circles into the tins and prick the bases with a fork.

2 Combine the corn, cheese and capsicum in a bowl and season. Whisk the eggs, buttermilk, cream, mustard and Tabasco sauce.

3 Spoon some of the vegetable mixture into the pastry cases, then pour the egg mixture over the top until the cases are almost full. Bake for 20–25 minutes, or until set. Serve cold.

# chicken sausage rolls

### MAKES 36

3 frozen puff pastry sheets, thawed

2 eggs, lightly beaten

750 g (1 lb 10 oz) minced (ground) chicken

4 spring onions (scallions), finely chopped

80 g (2¾ oz/1 cup) fresh breadcrumbs

1 carrot, finely grated

2 tablespoons fruit chutney

1 tablespoon sweet chilli sauce

1 tablespoon grated fresh ginger

sesame seeds, to sprinkle

1 Preheat the oven to 200°C (400°F/Gas 6). Lightly grease two baking trays.

2 Cut the pastry sheets in half and lightly brush the edges with some of the beaten egg.

3 Mix half the remaining egg with the remaining ingredients, except the sesame seeds, in a large bowl, then divide into six even portions.

4 Pipe or spoon the filling down the centre of each piece of pastry, then brush the edges with some of the egg.

5 Fold the pastry over the filling, overlapping the edges and placing the join underneath.

6 Brush the rolls with more egg. Sprinkle with sesame seeds, then cut each into six short pieces. Cut two small slashes on top of each roll.

7 Place on the baking trays and bake for 15 minutes. Reduce the heat to 180°C (350°F/Gas 4) and bake for another 15 minutes, or until puffed and golden.

# vegie puffs

**MAKES 12**

1 potato, peeled and finely chopped

1 carrot, finely chopped

1 zucchini (courgette), peeled and chopped

1 celery stalk, chopped

40 g (1½ oz/¼ cup) chopped pumpkin (squash)

30 g (1 oz/¼ cup) chopped broccoli

30 g (1 oz/¼ cup) chopped cauliflower

250 g (9 oz/2 cups) grated tasty cheese

1 sheet puff pastry, thawed, cut in half

milk, for coating

1 Put the potato, carrot, zucchini, celery, pumpkin, broccoli and cauliflower in a small saucepan and add enough water to cover. Bring to the boil, then reduce the heat and simmer for 3 minutes. Drain well and transfer to a bowl to cool. Add the cheese to the vegetables and mix well.

2 Preheat the oven to 220°C (425°F/Gas 7). Put the two pieces of pastry out on a board, divide the mixture in half and spread it along the long side of each piece.

3 Roll up the pastry to form a sausage shape, brush the edge with a little milk and press to seal. Place, seam side down, on a cutting board.

4 Cut each roll into six even-sized pieces using a sharp knife. Make a small slit in the centre of each and place on a lightly greased baking tray. Brush with milk and bake for 10 minutes or until crisp and golden.

# sunken subs

4 hot dog rolls

20 g (¾ oz) butter

1 garlic clove, crushed

440 g (15½ oz) tinned spaghetti in tomato and cheese sauce

80 g (2¾ oz) sliced ham, chopped

100 g (3½ oz) cheddar cheese slices, cut into strips

1. Preheat the oven to 180°C (350°F/Gas 4). Brush a baking tray with oil.

2. Cut the hot dog rolls in half horizontally. Place on the baking tray.

3. Heat the butter in a saucepan. Add the garlic and cook for 2–3 minutes. Brush a little on each roll half. Top with spaghetti, ham and cheese.

4. Bake for 12 minutes, or until the cheese melts.

# ham and pineapple pizza wheels

MAKES 16

250 g (9 oz/2 cups) self-raising flour

40 g (1½ oz) butter, chopped

125 ml (4 fl oz/½ cup) milk

90 g (3¼ oz/⅓ cup) tomato paste (concentrated purée)

2 small onions, finely chopped

4 pineapple slices, finely chopped

200 g (7 oz) sliced ham, shredded

80 g (2¾ oz) cheddar cheese, grated

2 tablespoons finely chopped flat-leaf (Italian) parsley

1. Preheat the oven to 180°C (350°F/Gas 4). Brush two baking trays with oil.

2. Sift the flour into a bowl. Rub in the butter using your fingers. Make a well in the centre and add almost all the milk. Mix until the mixture comes together in beads. Gather into a ball and turn out onto a lightly floured surface.

3. Divide the dough in half. Roll out each half on baking paper to make a 20 x 30 cm (8 x 12 inch) rectangle, about 5 mm (¼ inch) thick. Spread the tomato paste over each rectangle, leaving a 1 cm (½ inch) border.

4. Mix the onion, pineapple, ham, cheddar and parsley together. Spread over the tomato paste, leaving a 2 cm (¾ inch) border. Roll up each rectangle along the long edge.

5. Cut each roll into eight even slices. Place the slices on the baking trays. Bake for 20 minutes, or until golden.

# frankfurt bonbons

**MAKES 12**

12 small good-quality cocktail frankfurts

3 sheets frozen puff pastry, thawed

1 egg, lightly beaten

cotton or jute string

1 Preheat the oven to 180°C (350°F/Gas 4). Line two baking trays with baking paper.

2 Prick the frankfurts with a fork. Cut each pastry sheet into four squares. Brush each square with beaten egg.

3 Place a frankfurt on each pastry square and roll it up. Gently press the edges together.

4 Carefully pinch in the ends of the pastry. Tie the ends loosely with pieces of string.

5 Place the pastries on the trays. Brush lightly with the beaten egg. Bake for 15 minutes, or until golden. Remind your party guests not to eat the string!

# mini galactic pizzas

**MAKES 40**

250 g (9 oz/2 cups) self-raising flour

100 g (3½ oz) butter, chopped

125 ml (4 fl oz/½ cup) buttermilk

2 tablespoons tomato paste (concentrated purée)

1 cabanossi stick, thinly sliced

1 small onion, thinly sliced

10 cherry tomatoes, thinly sliced

6 cheddar cheese slices, cut into 3 cm (1¼ inch) rounds

1　Preheat the oven to 180°C (350°F/Gas 4). Line two large baking trays with foil and grease.

2　Combine the flour and butter in a food processor. Process for 30 seconds or until the mixture is crumbly. Add the buttermilk. Process for 30 seconds.

3　Knead the dough on a floured surface until smooth. Roll the dough out to 3 mm (⅛ inch) thick. Cut into rounds using a 5 cm (2 inch) round cutter.

4　Place the rounds on the tray and spread with the tomato paste. Arrange the cabanossi, onion and tomato on top, then top with the cheese. Bake for 10 minutes, or until crisp.

# chicken and corn bites

**MAKES 50**

185 g (6½ oz/1½ cups) self-raising flour

2 teaspoons chicken stock (bouillon) powder

½ teaspoon chicken seasoning salt

60 g (2¼ oz) butter, chopped

50 g (1¾ oz) corn chips, finely crushed

2 eggs, lightly beaten

chicken seasoning salt, extra, to sprinkle

1　Preheat the oven to 180°C (350°F/Gas 4). Line two baking trays with baking paper.

2　Sift the flour, stock powder and seasoning salt into a large bowl and add the butter. Rub into the flour with your fingertips until the mixture resembles fine breadcrumbs. Stir in the corn chips. Make a well in the centre, add the eggs and mix until the mixture comes together in beads.

3　Gently gather the dough together, lift out onto a lightly floured surface and press together into a ball. Roll out to 5 mm (¼ inch) thick.

4　Cut the dough into shapes with a plain or fluted cookie cutter. Place on the tray and sprinkle with the chicken salt. Bake for 15 minutes, or until lightly browned.

# pizza margherita

**SERVES 4**

4 mini pizza bases

**topping**

1 tablespoon olive oil

425 g (15 oz) tinned crushed tomatoes

1 bay leaf

1 teaspoon chopped thyme

6 chopped basil leaves

150 g (5½ oz) bocconcini cheese (fresh baby mozzarella cheese), thinly sliced

olive oil, extra, to drizzle

1 Preheat the oven to 210°C (415°F/Gas 6–7).

2 To make the topping, heat the oil in a saucepan over medium heat. Add the tomatoes, bay leaf, thyme and basil and simmer, stirring occasionally, for about 20–25 minutes, or until thick. Leave to cool, then remove the bay leaf.

3 Lightly grease two baking trays. Sprinkle the trays with flour and place the bases on top.

4 Spread the sauce over the pizza bases, leaving a 3 cm (1¼ inch) border.

5 Arrange the bocconcini over the top and drizzle with olive oil. Bake for 15 minutes, or until crisp and bubbling. Serve warm.

# muffins, cupcakes and cookies

# lemon meringue muffins

### MAKES 12

330 g (11³⁄₄ oz/1³⁄₄ cups) self-raising flour

185 g (6¹⁄₂ oz/³⁄₄ cup) caster (superfine) sugar

1 egg

1 egg yolk

170 ml (5¹⁄₂ fl oz/²⁄₃ cup) milk

¹⁄₂ teaspoon vanilla extract

90 g (3¹⁄₄ oz) unsalted butter, melted and cooled

200 g (7 oz/²⁄₃ cup) ready-made lemon curd

3 egg whites

1. Preheat the oven to 200°C (400°F/Gas 6). Grease 12 standard muffin holes.

2. Sift the flour into a large bowl and stir in 60 g (2¹⁄₄ oz/¹⁄₄ cup) of the caster sugar. Make a well in the centre.

3. Put a pinch of salt, the egg and egg yolk in a bowl and beat together. Stir in the milk, vanilla and butter. Pour into the well. Fold until just combined.

4. Divide the muffin mixture among the holes. Bake for 15 minutes. Cool in the tin for 10 minutes.

5. Hollow out the centre of each muffin with a knife.

6. Spoon the lemon curd into the muffin holes.

7. Whisk the egg whites until firm peaks form. Add the remaining sugar, beating well after each addition.

8. Reduce the oven to 150°C (300°F/Gas 2). Put a heaped tablespoon of meringue on top of each muffin. Sprinkle over a little caster sugar. Bake for 5–7 minutes, or until crisp. Cool in the tin for 10 minutes, then transfer to a wire rack.

# banana muffins with caramel syrup

**MAKES 12**

250 g (9 oz/2 cups) self-raising flour

125 g (4½ oz/½ cup) caster (superfine) sugar

250 ml (9 fl oz/1 cup) milk

1 egg

2 teaspoons vanilla extract

75 g (2½ oz) unsalted butter, melted and cooled

240 g (8½ oz/1 cup) mashed banana

300 g (10½ oz) sugar

1 Preheat the oven to 200°C (400°F/Gas 6). Grease 12 standard muffin holes.

2 Sift the flour into a bowl and stir in the caster sugar. Make a well in the centre.

3 Put the milk, egg and vanilla in a bowl. Whisk and pour into the well.

4 Add the butter and banana. Fold until combined—the batter should be lumpy.

5 Divide among the muffin holes. Bake for about 20–25 minutes, or until lightly golden.

6 To make the syrup, put the sugar and about 100 ml (3½ fl oz) of water in a small saucepan over medium heat and stir until the sugar dissolves. Increase the heat and cook for 8 minutes, or until golden. Remove from heat and add 4 tablespoons of water (careful—it will spit). Stir the water into the caramel until smooth.

7 Cool in the tin for 5 minutes, then transfer to a wire rack. Drizzle with the syrup.

# berry cheesecake muffins

### MAKES 6

215 g (7½ oz/1¾ cups) self-raising flour

2 eggs, lightly beaten

3 tablespoons oil

2 tablespoons raspberry jam

60 g (2¼ oz/¼ cup) mixed berry yoghurt

125 g (4½ oz/½ cup) caster (superfine) sugar

60 g (2¼ oz) cream cheese

1 tablespoon raspberry jam, extra, for filling

icing (confectioners') sugar, sifted, to dust

1 Preheat the oven to 180°C (350°F/Gas 4). Lightly grease six standard muffin holes.

2 Sift the flour into a large bowl and make a well in the centre. Place the eggs, oil, jam, yoghurt and sugar in a separate bowl and combine. Add to the sifted flour. Mix the batter until just combined.

3 Spoon three-quarters of the mixture into the muffin holes. Cut the cream cheese into six equal portions and place a portion on the centre of each muffin. Spread the tops with jam and cover with remaining muffin batter.

4 Bake for 30 minutes, or until lightly golden. Turn out onto a wire rack to cool. Dust with icing sugar to serve.

**Note:** These muffins are best eaten as soon as they are cool enough.

# apple and cinnamon muffins

### MAKES 12

300 g (10½ oz/2 cups) self-raising flour

140 g (5 oz/¾ cup, lightly packed) soft brown sugar

1 teaspoon cinnamon

160 ml (5¼ fl oz/⅔ cup) milk

4 tablespoons canola oil

2 eggs, whisked

2 ripe apples, peeled, grated

1 Preheat the oven to 180°C (350°F/Gas 4). Lightly grease twelve 80 ml (2½ fl oz/⅓ cup) muffin holes.

2 Sift the flour, sugar and cinnamon into a large bowl.

3 In a separate bowl, combine the milk, oil and eggs. Add the milk mixture and apples to the flour mixture. Mix until just combined. Spoon evenly among the muffin holes.

4 Bake for 18–20 minutes, or until lightly golden. Leave for 5 minutes, then turn out onto a wire rack to cool.

# almond, berry and yoghurt muffins

### MAKES 12

185g (6½ oz/1½ cups) plain (all-purpose) flour

3 teaspoons baking powder

115 g (4 oz/1 cup) ground almonds

185g (6½ oz/¾ cup) caster (superfine) sugar

2 eggs

125 g (4½ oz) unsalted butter, melted, cooled

250g (9 oz/1 cup) plain (all-purpose) yoghurt

300 g (10½ oz) blueberries or raspberries

2 tablespoons flaked almonds

1 Preheat the oven to 180°C (350°F/Gas 4). Grease 12 standard muffin holes.

2 Sift the flour and baking powder into a large bowl and stir in the ground almonds and sugar. Make a well in the centre.

3 Put the eggs, butter and yoghurt in a bowl, whisk and pour into the well. Fold gently until well combined — the batter should be lumpy.

4 Fold in the berries. Divide the mixture among the muffin holes. Top each muffin with flaked almonds.

5 Bake for 20 minutes, or until lightly golden. Cool for 5 minutes, then transfer to a wire rack.

# chocolate muffins

### MAKES 12

310 g (11 oz/2½ cups) self-raising flour

40 g (1½ oz/⅓ cup) unsweetened cocoa powder

½ teaspoon bicarbonate of soda (baking soda)

180 g (6 oz/⅔ cup) caster (superfine) sugar

375 ml (12 fl oz/1½ cups) buttermilk

2 eggs

150 g (5½ oz) unsalted butter, melted and cooled

60 g (2¼ oz) chocolate, grated

1 Preheat the oven to 200°C (400°F/Gas 6). Grease 12 standard muffin holes.

2 Sift the flour, cocoa and bicarbonate of soda into a bowl and add the sugar. Make a well in the centre.

3 Whisk the buttermilk and eggs together and pour into the well. Add the butter and fold gently with a metal spoon until just combined. Do not overmix. Fill each muffin hole about three-quarters full.

4 Bake for 20–25 minutes, or until the muffins are risen. Cool for 2 minutes, then transfer to a wire rack. Sprinkle the grated chocolate on top while still warm.

# rhubarb and custard muffins

### MAKES 12

185 g (6½ oz/¾ cup) caster (superfine) sugar

300 g (10½ oz) chopped rhubarb

280 g (2¼ cups) self-raising flour

90 g (3¼ oz/¾ cup) custard powder

125 g (4½ oz/½ cup) caster (superfine) sugar

1 egg

30 g (1 oz) unsalted butter, melted and cooled

250 ml (9 fl oz/1 cup) skim milk

1 Preheat the oven to 200°C (400°F/Gas 6). Grease 12 standard muffin holes.

2 Combine the caster sugar and 250 ml (9 fl oz/1 cup) of water in a saucepan and stir over medium heat. Add the rhubarb and cook over low heat for 2 minutes, or until tender. Transfer to a bowl and cool. Drain, being careful not to break up the rhubarb.

3 Sift the self-raising flour and custard powder into a bowl. Stir in the caster sugar.

4 Combine the egg, butter and milk and add to the dry ingredients. Fold until combined. Fold in the rhubarb.

5 Divide the mixture among the muffin holes. Sprinkle with sugar and bake for 20 minutes, or until golden. Cool for 5 minutes, then transfer to a wire rack.

# pear and muesli muffins

## MAKES 12

225 g (8 oz/1½ cups) toasted muesli

1 tablespoon plain (all-purpose) flour

125 g (4½ oz/½ cup) caster (superfine) sugar

90 g (3¼ oz) unsalted butter, melted

100 g (3½ oz/½ cup) chopped dried pears

125 ml (4 fl oz/½ cup) orange juice

1 tablespoon finely grated orange zest

250 g (9 oz/2 cups) self-raising flour

½ teaspoon baking powder

250 ml (9 fl oz/1 cup) buttermilk

3 tablespoons milk

90 g (3¼ oz/¼ cup) honey

1. To make the topping, place 75 g (2½ oz/½ cup) of the muesli, the plain flour and half the sugar in a small bowl and mix in 2 tablespoons of the butter.

2. Preheat the oven to 200°C (400°F/Gas 6). Grease 12 standard muffin holes. Put the pears in a bowl and add the orange juice and zest. Leave for 10 minutes.

3. Sift the self-raising flour and baking powder into the bowl with the pears. Add the remaining muesli and sugar. Make a well in the centre.

4. Whisk the buttermilk and milk together and add to the pear mixture. Combine the honey and remaining butter, then add to the pear mixture. Mix well.

5. Divide the batter among the muffin holes, then sprinkle on the topping. Bake for 25–30 minutes, or until cooked. Cool briefly, then transfer to a wire rack.

# apple and orange mini cakes

**MAKES 24**

90 g (3¼ oz) unsalted butter

125 g (4½ oz/⅔ cup) soft brown sugar

1 tablespoon honey

1 egg

270 g (9½ oz/1 cup) apple purée

125 g (4½ oz/1 cup) wholemeal (whole-wheat) self-raising flour

60 g (2¼ oz/½ cup) self-raising flour

1 teaspoon ground cinnamon

pinch of powdered cloves

**orange glaze icing**

125 g (4½ oz/1 cup) icing (confectioners') sugar

10 g (¼ oz) unsalted butter

1 teaspoon grated orange zest

2 tablespoons orange juice

1 Preheat the oven to 180°C (350°F/Gas 4). Grease 24 mini muffin holes. Beat the butter, sugar and honey together until light and creamy, then add the egg and apple purée and beat until well combined.

2 Sift in the flours and spices and mix well. Spoon the mixture into the muffin holes and bake for 20 minutes. Allow to cool.

3 To make the icing, mix the icing sugar, butter, orange zest and orange juice in a heatproof bowl. Place over a saucepan of simmering water and stir until smooth. Allow to cool slightly, then ice the cakes.

# individual milk chocolate cakes

**MAKES 6**

75 g (2³/4 oz) unsalted butter

75 g (2³/4 oz) milk chocolate, chopped

80 g (2³/4 oz/¹/3 cup) brown sugar

2 eggs, lightly beaten

60 g (2¹/4 oz/¹/2 cup) self-raising flour, sifted

silver cachous, to decorate

**ganache**

80 g (2³/4 oz) milk chocolate, chopped

2 tablespoons thick (double/heavy) cream

1. Preheat the oven to 160°C (315°F/Gas 2–3). Line a flat-bottomed 6-hole cupcake tray with paper patty cases.

2. Put the butter and chocolate in a heatproof bowl and place over a saucepan of simmering water, making sure the base of the bowl doesn't touch the water. Stir until melted. Remove from the heat, add the sugar and egg and mix. Stir in the flour.

3. Transfer the mixture to a measuring jug and pour into the patty cases.

4. Bake for 20–25 minutes, or until cooked. Leave in the tin for 10 minutes, then transfer to a wire rack to cool.

5. To make the ganache, place the chocolate and cream in a heatproof bowl. Place over a saucepan of simmering water. Stir until melted. Allow to cool for about 8 minutes, or until thickened slightly.

6. Spread a heaped teaspoon of ganache over the top of each cake. Decorate with silver cachous.

# individual white chocolate chip cakes

## MAKES 12

125 g (4½ oz) unsalted butter, softened

185 g (6½ oz/¾ cup) caster (superfine) sugar

2 eggs, lightly beaten

1 teaspoon vanilla extract

250 g (9 oz/2 cups) self-raising flour, sifted

125 ml (4 fl oz/½ cup) buttermilk

250 g (9 oz) white chocolate chips

white chocolate, shaved, to decorate

**white chocolate cream cheese icing (frosting)**

100 g (3½ oz) white chocolate

3 tablespoons thick (double/heavy) cream

200 g (7 oz/¾ cup) cream cheese, softened

40 g (1½ oz/⅓ cup) icing (confectioners') sugar

1 Preheat the oven to 170°C (325°F/Gas 3). Grease 12 standard muffin holes.

2 Beat the butter and sugar in a large bowl using electric beaters until pale and creamy. Gradually add the egg, beating well after each addition. Add the vanilla extract and beat until combined.

3 Fold in the flour alternately with the buttermilk, then fold in the chocolate chips.

4 Spoon into the muffin holes until three-quarters full. Bake for 20 minutes, or until lightly golden. Leave in the tins for 5 minutes, then turn out onto a wire rack to cool.

5 To make the icing, melt the chocolate and cream in a small saucepan over low heat until smooth. Cool slightly, then add to the cream cheese and icing sugar and beat until smooth.

6 Spread the icing over the cakes and top with white chocolate shavings.

# strawberry and blueberry shortcakes

**MAKES 4**

**shortcake**
90 g (3¼ oz) butter
60 g (2¼ oz) sugar
1 egg
140 g (5 oz) plain (all-purpose) flour
2 teaspoons baking powder
a pinch of salt
4 tablespoons milk

whipped cream, to serve
250 g (9 oz) strawberries, quartered
150 g (5½ oz) blueberries
icing (confectioners') sugar, to dust

1 Preheat the oven to 180°C (350°F/Gas 4). Cream the butter with the sugar until light and creamy. Add the egg and mix well.

2 Sift in the flour, baking powder and salt, then add the milk. Fold well.

3 Roll out to 2 cm (¾ inch) thick on a well-floured surface. Cut into circles using 7.5 cm (3 inch) round cutter. Put the circles on a greased baking tray and bake for 20 minutes.

4 Cool slightly, then split and fill with cream and strawberries and blueberries. Dust with icing sugar to serve.

# strawberry muffins

**MAKES 18**

375 g (13 oz/3 cups) plain (all-purpose) flour
110 g (3¾ oz/½ cup) sugar
1 tablespoon baking powder
95 g (3¼ oz/½ cup) brown sugar
125 g (4½ oz) unsalted butter, melted
3 eggs
250 ml (9 fl oz/1 cup) milk
225 g (8 oz/1½ cups) strawberries, chopped

1 Preheat the oven to 200°C (400°F/Gas 6). Lightly grease 18 standard muffin holes.

2 Sift the flour, sugar and baking powder into a bowl. Stir in the brown sugar.

3 Combine the melted butter, eggs and milk. Stir into the dry ingredients until just blended.

4 Fold in the berries very lightly. Spoon into the muffin holes until three-quarters full.

5 Bake for 20 minutes, or until lightly golden. Serve hot with butter.

# fluffy coconut cupcakes

## MAKES 36

250 g (9 oz/2 cups) self-raising flour, sifted

45 g (1²/₃ oz/¹/₂ cup) desiccated coconut

230 g (8¹/₂ oz/1 cup) caster (superfine) sugar

250 ml (9 fl oz/1 cup) buttermilk

2 eggs, lightly beaten

1 teaspoon natural coconut extract

125 g (4¹/₂ oz) unsalted butter, melted

### coconut icing (frosting)

280 g (10 oz/2¹/₄ cups) icing (confectioners') sugar

135 g (4³/₄ oz/1¹/₂ cups) desiccated coconut

75 g (2¹/₂ oz) unsalted butter, softened

¹/₂ teaspoon natural coconut extract

2 tablespoons hot water

pink sugar crystals, to sprinkle

1 Preheat the oven to 180°C (350°F/Gas 4). Line 36 standard muffin holes with paper patty cases.

2 Combine the flour, coconut and sugar in a bowl and make a well in the centre.

3 Combine the buttermilk, eggs, coconut extract and butter in a bowl. Add to the flour mixture and mix until combined.

4 Divide the mixture evenly among the cases. Bake for 12 minutes, or until a skewer comes out clean when inserted into the centre of a cake. Transfer onto a wire rack to cool.

5 To make the coconut icing, combine the icing sugar and coconut in a bowl. Add the butter, coconut extract and enough hot water to make an icing that will be easy to spread.

6 Decorate each cake with a thick covering of icing and sprinkle with pink sugar crystals.

# jelly dipped cupcakes

### MAKES 30

250 g (9 oz/2 cups) self-raising flour

165 g (5³/₄ oz/³/₄ cup) sugar

125 g (4¹/₂ oz) unsalted butter, softened

3 eggs

3 tablespoons milk

¹/₂ teaspoon vanilla extract

**icing (frosting)**

125 g (4¹/₂ oz/1 cup) icing (confectioners') sugar

red and green food colouring

**jelly**

85 g (3 oz) packet of red jelly crystals

85 g (3 oz) packet green jelly crystals

400 ml (14 fl oz) boiling water

180 g (6 oz/2 cups) desiccated coconut, to coat

1 Preheat the oven to 180°C (350°F/Gas 4). Line 18 standard muffin holes with paper patty cases.

2 Sift the flour and sugar into a bowl. Add the butter, eggs, milk and vanilla and beat until smooth. Fill the patty cases three-quarters full with the mixture.

3 Bake for 15 minutes, or until golden. Remove from the muffin holes and place onto a wire rack to cool.

4 To make the icing, mix the icing sugar and 1–2 tablespoons of water, until thick. Divide among separate bowls and add red food colouring to one bowl and green to the other.

5 Put jelly crystals into separate bowls. Pour half of the boiling water into each bowl and stir to dissolve. Allow to cool, but not to set.

6 Dip each cake into either green or red jelly. Roll the cakes in the coconut. Refrigerate overnight to set. Serve chilled.

# fairy cakes

## MAKES 12

120 g (4¼ oz) unsalted butter, softened

145 g (5½ oz/⅔ cup) caster (superfine) sugar

185 g (6½ oz/1½ cups) self-raising flour

125 ml (4 fl oz/½ cup) milk

2 teaspoons vanilla extract

2 eggs

125 ml (4 fl oz/½ cup) pouring (whipping) cream

105 g (3¾ oz/⅓ cup) strawberry jam

icing (confectioners') sugar, to dust

1 Preheat the oven to 180°C (350°F/Gas 4). Line 12 standard muffin holes with paper patty cases.

2 Beat the butter, sugar, flour, milk, vanilla and eggs in a bowl using electric beaters on low speed for about 2 minutes. Increase the speed and beat for 2 minutes, or until smooth and pale.

3 Divide the mixture evenly among the cases. Bake for 20 minutes, or until lightly golden. Transfer to a wire rack to cool.

4 Whip the cream using electric beaters until soft peaks form.

5 Using a small sharp knife, cut shallow rounds from the top of each cake. Cut these in half. Spoon 2 teaspoons of the cream into the hole in each cake. Spread 1 teaspoon of the jam in the centre.

6 Position the two halves of the cake tops in the jam so they look like butterfly wings. Dust the cakes with icing sugar.

# cupcakes

## MAKES ABOUT 18

250 g (9 oz/2 cups) self-raising flour

165 g (5³/₄ oz/³/₄ cup) sugar

125 g (4¹/₂ oz) unsalted butter, softened

3 eggs

3 tablespoons milk

¹/₂ teaspoon vanilla extract

**icing**

90 g (3¹/₄ oz/³/₄ cup) icing (confectioners') sugar

1 teaspoon unsweetened cocoa powder

20 g (³/₄ oz) unsalted butter, softened

chocolate melts (buttons), to decorate

1 Preheat the oven to 180°C (350°F/Gas 4). Put 18 paper patty cases in standard muffin holes.

2 Sift the flour and sugar into a mixing bowl. Add the butter, eggs, milk and vanilla and beat until smooth. Fill the patty cases three-quarters full with the mixture.

3 Bake for 15 minutes, or until the cupcakes are golden. Cool on a wire rack.

4 To make the icing, mix the icing sugar, cocoa and butter with a little hot water until smooth. Spread over the cakes. Top each cake with a chocolate melt.

# anzac biscuits

## MAKES ABOUT 25

200 g (7 oz/2 cups) rolled (porridge) oats

125 g (4½ oz/1 cup) plain (all-purpose) flour

180 g (6½ oz/2 cups) desiccated coconut

350 g (12 oz/1½ cups) caster (superfine) sugar

250 g (9 oz) unsalted butter

4 tablespoons golden syrup or honey

1 teaspoon bicarbonate of soda (baking soda)

1 Preheat the oven to 160°C (315°F/Gas 2–3). Lightly grease two baking trays. Put the oats, flour, coconut and sugar in a large mixing bowl.

2 Melt the butter and golden syrup in a saucepan, stirring. Take off the heat.

3 Mix the baking soda and 2 tablespoons of boiling water in a cup. Add to the melted butter in the saucepan. Add to the bowl and mix well to combine.

4 Roll tablespoons of the mixture into balls. Put on trays spacing them 5 cm (2 inches) apart. Press lightly with a fork. Bake for 20 minutes, one tray at a time, until golden and crisp.

# melting moments

## MAKES ABOUT 45

40 g (1½ oz/⅓ cup) cornflour (cornstarch)

125 g (4½ oz/1 cup) plain (all-purpose) flour

180 g (6½ oz) unsalted butter

40 g (1½ oz/⅓ cup) icing (confectioners') sugar

1 teaspoon vanilla extract

100 g (3½ oz) glacé cherries, halved

1 Preheat the oven to 180°C (350°F/Gas 4). Line two baking trays with baking paper.

2 Sift the cornflour and plain flour into a bowl.

3 Put the butter, sugar and vanilla into a mixing bowl and beat with electric beaters until light and creamy.

4 Using a flat-bladed knife, stir the sifted flours into the butter mixture until just combined and the mixture is smooth.

5 Spoon teaspoons of the mixture onto the trays, leaving room for spreading.

6 Top each biscuit with half a cherry and bake for 15 minutes, or until lightly golden and crisp.

7 Transfer the biscuits to a wire rack to cool.

# teddy bear cakes

**MAKES 12**

340 g (12 oz) packet butter cake mix

100 g (3½ oz) dark chocolate chips

310 g (11 oz/1 cup) chocolate hazelnut spread

250 g (9 oz) honey-flavoured mini teddy biscuits

2 tablespoons sprinkles

1  Preheat the oven to 180°C (350°F/ Gas 4). Lightly grease 12 standard muffin holes with oil.

2  Prepare the butter cake mix according to the directions on the packet. Fold the chocolate chips through the mixture.

3  Spoon the mixture into the prepared holes. Bake for 15 minutes, or until firm and golden brown. Allow to stand in the tin for 5 minutes. Remove the cakes and cool on a wire rack.

4  Spread each cake with the chocolate hazelnut spread. Place five teddy biscuits around the edge of the cakes. Decorate with sprinkles.

# mini marble cakes

**SERVES 6**

1 teaspoon natural vanilla extract

185 g (6½ oz) unsalted butter, chopped

230 g (8 oz/1 cup) caster (superfine) sugar

3 eggs

280 g (10 oz/2¼ cups) self-raising flour

185 ml (6 fl oz/¾ cup) milk

2 tablespoons unsweetened cocoa powder

1½ tablespoons warm milk, extra

1 Preheat the oven to 200°C (400°F/ Gas 6). Lightly grease eight mini loaf (bar) tins and line the bases with baking paper.

2 Combine the vanilla extract, butter and sugar in a bowl and beat using electric beaters until fluffy. Add the eggs one at a time, beating well after each addition. Sift the flour, then fold it into the creamed mixture with the milk. Divide the mixture in half and put the second half into a clean bowl.

3 Combine the cocoa powder and warm milk in a bowl and stir until smooth, then add to one half of the cake mixture, stirring. Spoon the two mixtures into the tin in alternate spoonfuls. Using a skewer, cut through the mixture four times to create a marble effect.

4 Bake for 50–60 minutes. Leave in the tin for 5 minutes, then turn out onto a wire rack to cool.

# passionfruit melting moments

### MAKES 14

250 g (9 oz) unsalted butter, softened

40 g (1¹/₂ oz/¹/₃ cup) icing (confectioners') sugar

1 teaspoon vanilla extract

185 g (6¹/₂ oz/1¹/₂ cups) self-raising flour

60 g (2¹/₄ oz/¹/₂ cup) custard powder

**passionfruit filling**

60 g (2¹/₄ oz) unsalted butter

60 g (2¹/₄ oz/¹/₂ cup) icing (confectioners') sugar

1¹/₂ tablespoons passionfruit pulp

1  Preheat the oven to 180°C (350°F/Gas 4). Line two baking trays with baking paper.

2  Beat the butter and sugar using electric beaters until light and creamy. Beat in the vanilla extract. Sift in the flour and custard powder and mix to a soft dough.

3  Roll level tablespoons of the mixture into 28 balls and place on the trays.

4  Flatten slightly with a floured fork. Bake for about 20 minutes, or until lightly golden. Allow to cool on a wire rack.

5  To make the filling, beat the butter and sugar using electric beaters until light and creamy, then beat in the passionfruit pulp.

6  Use the filling to sandwich the biscuits together. Leave to firm before serving.

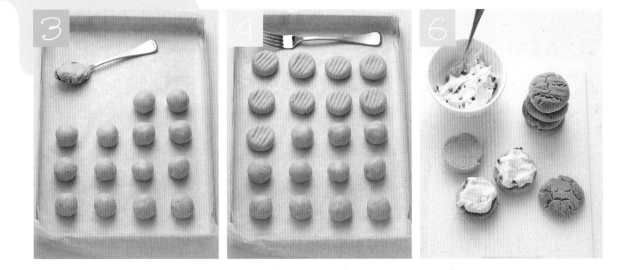

## coconut cookies

### MAKES ABOUT 45

125 g (4$^{1}$/$_{2}$ oz) unsalted butter

230 g (8 oz/1 cup) caster (superfine) sugar

1 egg

1 teaspoon vanilla extract

1 tablespoon white vinegar

65 g (2$^{1}$/$_{4}$ oz/$^{3}$/$_{4}$ cup) desiccated coconut

185 g (6$^{1}$/$_{2}$ oz/1$^{1}$/$_{2}$ cups) self-raising flour

90 g (3$^{1}$/$_{4}$ oz/1 cup) desiccated coconut, extra

1  Preheat the oven to 180°C (350°F/Gas 4). Lightly grease a baking tray.

2  Beat the butter, sugar, egg and vanilla until smooth. Stir the vinegar into the bowl. Add the coconut. Sift in the flour. Mix well.

3  Roll teaspoonfuls of mixture into balls. Toss each ball in extra coconut.

4  Place 5 cm (2 inches) apart on the baking tray. Bake for 15 minutes, or until golden. Allow to cool on a wire rack.

## munchy oatmeals

### MAKES 28

125 g (4$^{1}$/$_{2}$ oz/1 cup) plain (all-purpose) flour

140 g (5 oz/$^{2}$/$_{3}$ cup) sugar

100 g (3$^{1}$/$_{2}$ oz/1 cup) rolled oats

90 g (3$^{1}$/$_{4}$ oz/1 cup) desiccated coconut

125 g (4$^{1}$/$_{2}$ oz) unsalted butter

3 tablespoons golden syrup or honey

$^{1}$/$_{2}$ teaspoon bicarbonate of soda (baking soda)

1  Preheat the oven to 180°C (350°F/Gas 4). Lightly grease two 28 x 32 cm (11¼ x 12½ inch) baking trays and line with baking paper.

2  Sift the flour and sugar into a large bowl. Add the oats and coconut, and make a well in the centre.

3  Combine the butter and golden syrup in a small saucepan. Stir over low heat until smooth, then remove from the heat. Dissolve the bicarbonate of soda in 1 tablespoon of boiling water and add to the butter mixture, which will foam up instantly. Add to the dry ingredients. Stir until well combined.

4  Roll level tablespoonfuls of mixture into rough balls and place onto the prepared trays, allowing room for spreading. Flatten gently with your fingers.

5  Bake for 20 minutes, or until just golden. Transfer to a wire rack to cool.

# shortbreads

**MAKES 16**

250 g (9 oz/2 cups) plain (all-purpose) flour

2 tablespoons rice flour

115 (4 oz/1/2 cup) caster (superfine) sugar

250 g (9 oz) unsalted butter, chopped

1 Preheat the oven to 160°C (315°F/Gas 2–3). Lightly grease two baking trays.

2 Sift the flours together into a large bowl and mix in the sugar. Rub in the butter using your fingertips. Turn out onto a floured surface and knead gently.

3 Press out into a round about 1 cm (1/2 inch) thick. Cut out squares with a 7.5 cm (2 3/4 inch) square cutter, or any shaped cutters you have.

4 Bake for 25–30 minutes, or until lightly golden. Leave to cool on the trays for 5 minutes, then put on a wire rack to cool completely.

# lemon stars

**MAKES ABOUT 22**

125 g (4 1/2 oz) unsalted butter, cubed and softened

125 g (4 1/2 oz/1/2 cup) caster (superfine) sugar

2 egg yolks

2 teaspoons finely grated lemon zest

155 g (5 1/2 oz/1 1/4 cups) plain (all-purpose) flour

110 g (3 3/4 oz/3/4 cup) coarse cornmeal

icing (confectioners') sugar, to dust

1 Preheat the oven to 160°C (315°F/Gas 2–3). Line a baking tray with baking paper.

2 Beat the butter and sugar using electric beaters until creamy. Mix in the egg yolks, lemon zest, flour and cornmeal until it becomes a ball of soft dough.

3 Roll out on a lightly floured surface to 1 cm (1/2 inch) thick. Cut out stars using a 3 cm (1 1/4 inch) star-shaped cutter.

4 Bake for 15–20 minutes, or until lightly golden. Cool on a wire rack, then dust with the icing sugar.

# apricot cookies

## MAKES ABOUT 50

160 g (5½ oz) unsalted butter, cubed

185 g (6½ oz/¾ cup) caster (superfine) sugar

2 tablespoons marmalade

1 teaspoon vanilla extract

200 g (7 oz) dried apricots, chopped

125 g (4½ oz/1 cup) self-raising flour

40 g (1½ oz/⅓ cup) plain (all-purpose) flour

**lemon icing (frosting)**

250 g (9 oz/2 cups) icing (confectioners') sugar, sifted

2 teaspoons lemon juice

1 Line two baking trays with baking paper. Beat the butter and sugar until creamy. Add the marmalade, vanilla and apricots and mix.

2 Stir in the combined sifted flours. Turn out onto a floured surface and knead until smooth. Divide in half.

3 Place each portion onto a sheet of baking paper and roll up in the paper to form logs 25 cm (10 inches) long. Refrigerate for 15 minutes, or until firm.

4 Preheat the oven to 180°C (350°F/Gas 4). Cut the logs into 1 cm (½ inch) slices. Place on the trays. Bake for 10 minutes, or until golden. Cool on a wire rack.

5 To make the icing, combine the icing sugar, lemon juice and 3 teaspoons of hot water. Put in a piping bag. Pipe stripes over the cookies.

# animal biscuits

**MAKES ABOUT 30**

125 g (4¹/₂ oz) unsalted butter, softened

70 g (2¹/₂ oz) soft brown sugar

125 g (4¹/₂ oz) plain (all-purpose) flour

45 g (1¹/₂ oz) rice flour

¹/₄ teaspoon mixed (pumpkin pie) spice

1   Preheat the oven to 160°C (315°F/ Gas 2–3). Line two baking trays with baking paper.

2   Cream the butter and sugar in a bowl using electric beaters until fluffy. Add the sifted flours, spice and a pinch of salt and mix with a knife to a soft dough. Gather together and gently knead for 1 minute. Wrap in plastic wrap and refrigerate for 20 minutes.

3   Divide the mixture into four, then gently knead. Roll a portion onto a lightly floured surface to a thickness of 5 mm (¹/₄ inch).

4   Cut out shapes using biscuit cutters. Re-roll the trimmings and repeat the kneading, rolling and cutting with the left-over portions of dough. Put the shapes on the prepared trays

5   Bake for 10–15 minutes, or until lightly golden. Remove from the oven and leave to cool for 2 minutes, then transfer to a wire rack to cool. Store in an airtight container.

**Note:** If you don't have decorative cutters, you can cut into 5 cm (2 inch) rounds.

# biscuits with passionfruit icing and coconut ice topping

**MAKES ABOUT 50**

### biscuits (cookies)

125 g (4¹/2 oz) unsalted butter, cubed

125 g (4¹/2 oz/¹/2 cup) caster (superfine) sugar

1 egg

¹/4 teaspoon vanilla extract

125 g (4¹/2 oz/1 cup) plain (all-purpose) flour

125 g (4¹/2 oz/1 cup) self-raising flour

### passionfruit glacé icing (frosting)

155 g (5¹/2 oz/1¹/4 cups) sifted icing (confectioners') sugar

1 tablespoons fresh passionfruit pulp

### coconut ice topping

155 g (5¹/2 oz) icing (confectioners') sugar

1 tablespoon unsalted butter, softened

45 g (1¹/2 oz) desiccated coconut

¹/2 teaspoon vanilla extract

few drops pink food colouring

1. Preheat the oven to 160°C (315°F/ Gas 2–3). Line a baking tray with baking paper.

2. To make the biscuits, beat together the butter and caster sugar until creamy. Add the egg and vanilla extract and beat well. Sift the plain flour and self-raising flour and fold in to form a soft dough.

3. Turn out onto a sheet of baking paper, cover with another sheet and roll out to 5 mm (¹/4 inch) thick.

4. Using biscuit cutters, cut out assorted shapes and place on the tray. Bake in batches for 10–15 minutes, or until lightly golden.

5. Cool on a wire rack, then spread with your choice of topping.

6. To make the passionfruit icing, mix the icing sugar and fresh passionfruit pulp in a bowl. Stir over a saucepan of simmering water until smooth and glossy.

7. To make the coconut ice topping, mix the sifted icing sugar, butter, coconut, vanilla extract and food colouring in a bowl. Add 6–8 teaspoons of boiling water to make a thick, spreadable mixture.

**Note:** You can use these as toppings or to sandwich two biscuits together.

# snack bars

**MAKES 16–20**

60 g (2¼ oz/2 cups) puffed rice cereal

150 g (5½ oz/1½ cups) wholegrain rolled (porridge) oats

30 g (1 oz/¼ cup) sunflower seeds

40 g (1½ oz/¼ cup) sesame seeds

200 g (7 oz) packet dried fruit medley

40 g (1½ oz/⅓ cup) plain (all-purpose) flour

225 g (8 oz/½ cup) honey

45 g (1½ oz/¼ cup) brown sugar

1 Preheat the oven to 180°C (350°F/Gas 4). Line the base and two long sides of a 29 x 19 cm (11½ x 7½ inch) rectangular cake tin with baking paper.

2 Put the puffed rice cereal, oats, sunflower seeds, sesame seeds, dried fruit and flour in a bowl and mix.

3 Put the honey, sugar and 2 tablespoons of water in a small saucepan and heat over medium heat for 1–2 minutes. Stir the syrup into the dry ingredients.

4 Press the mixture firmly into the prepared tin. Use the back of a spoon to spread it evenly. Bake for 20 minutes, or until golden brown. Leave to cool in the tin, then lift out and cut into fingers.

# chocolate chip cookies

**MAKES ABOUT 22**

185 g (6½ oz/1½ cups) plain (all-purpose) flour

125 g (4½ oz/1 cup) unsweetened cocoa powder

280 g (10 oz/1½ cups) soft brown sugar

180 g (6½ oz) unsalted butter

150 g (5½ oz) dark chocolate, chopped

3 eggs, lightly beaten

170 g (6 oz/1 cup) dark choc chips

50 g (1¾ oz/⅓ cup) white choc chips

150 g (5½ oz) nuts of your choice, chopped (such as macadamias, pecans, almonds, brazils, walnuts or pistachios)

1 Preheat the oven to 180°C (350°F/ Gas 4). Line two baking trays with baking paper.

2 Sift the flour and cocoa into a bowl and stir in the sugar. Make a well in the centre.

3 Heat the butter and chocolate in a saucepan over low heat. Stir until the mixture is smooth.

4 Stir the butter mixture and eggs into the dry ingredients. Mix until well combined. Stir in the dark and white choc chips and the nuts.

5 Drop heaped tablespoons of the mixture onto the trays. Flatten each one slightly with your fingertips.

6 Bake for 15 minutes. Leave on the trays for at least 5 minutes before transferring to a wire rack to cool.

# crackle cookies

## MAKES ABOUT 60

125 g (4¹/₂ oz) unsalted butter, cubed and softened

370 g (13 oz/2 cups) soft brown sugar

1 teaspoon vanilla extract

2 eggs

60 g (2¹/₄ oz) dark chocolate, melted

4 tablespoons milk

340 g (11³/₄ oz/2³/₄ cups) plain (all-purpose) flour

2 tablespoons unsweetened cocoa powder

2 teaspoons baking powder

¹/₄ teaspoon ground allspice

85 g (3 oz/²/₃ cup) chopped pecan nuts

icing (confectioners') sugar, to coat

1 Lightly grease 2 baking trays. Beat the butter, sugar and vanilla until light and creamy. Beat in the eggs, one at a time. Stir the chocolate and milk into the butter mixture.

2 Sift the flour, cocoa, baking powder, allspice and a pinch of salt into the butter mixture and mix well. Stir the pecans through. Refrigerate for at least 3 hours, or overnight.

3 Preheat the oven to 180°C (350°F/Gas 4). Roll tablespoons of the mixture into balls and roll each in the icing sugar to coat.

4 Place well apart on the trays. Bake for 20–25 minutes, or until lightly browned. Leave for 3–4 minutes, then cool on a wire rack.

# honey snaps

**MAKES 24**

125 g (4½ oz/½ cup) unsalted butter, softened

55 g (2 oz/¼ cup) caster (superfine) sugar

45 g (1¾ oz/¼ cup) soft brown sugar

115 g (4 oz/⅓ cup) honey

1 egg yolk

1 teaspoon natural vanilla extract

250 g (9 oz/2 cups) plain (all-purpose) flour

½ teaspoon bicarbonate of soda (baking soda)

125 g (4½ oz/1 cup) icing (confectioners') sugar

1–2 tablespoons lemon juice

1. Preheat the oven to 180°C (350°F/ Gas 4). Line two baking trays with baking paper.

2. Cream the butter and caster and brown sugars in a bowl using electric beaters until fluffy. Add the honey, egg yolk and vanilla. Sift in the flour and bicarbonate of soda and stir to form a soft dough.

3. Shape tablespoons of the dough into circles. Place on the prepared trays and flatten slightly.

4. Bake for 10 minutes, or until golden. Cool on the trays for a few minutes, then transfer to a wire rack to cool.

5. To make the icing (frosting), place the icing sugar in a bowl. Add enough lemon juice until smooth. Spread the tops of the snaps with the icing.

# custard dream stars

**MAKES 30**

185 g (6$\frac{1}{2}$ oz/$\frac{3}{4}$ cup) unsalted
    butter, softened

40 g (1$\frac{1}{2}$ oz/$\frac{1}{3}$ cup) icing
    (confectioners') sugar

1 teaspoon natural vanilla extract

125 g (4$\frac{1}{2}$ oz/1 cup) plain
    (all-purpose) flour

40 g (1$\frac{1}{2}$ oz/$\frac{1}{3}$ cup) custard powder
    (instant vanilla pudding mix)

small coloured balls (cachous), to decorate

1  Preheat the oven to 180°C (350°F/
   Gas 4). Line two baking trays with
   baking paper.

2  Cream the butter, sugar and vanilla
   in a bowl using electric beaters
   until pale and fluffy. Sift in the flour
   and custard powder and stir with a
   wooden spoon to form a soft dough,
   being careful not to overmix.

3  Transfer the mixture to a piping
   (icing) bag fitted with a 1.5 cm
   ($\frac{5}{8}$ inch) star nozzle. Pipe the mixture
   well apart onto the prepared baking
   trays to form star shapes, about
   4 cm (1$\frac{1}{2}$ inches) in diameter.

4  Decorate each star with coloured
   balls. Refrigerate for 20 minutes.

5  Bake for 12–15 minutes, or until
   lightly golden. Allow to cool on the
   trays for a few minutes, then transfer
   to a wire rack to cool completely.

# caterpillar biscuits

**MAKES 25**

4 egg whites
230 g (8 oz/1 cup) caster (superfine) sugar
green and red food colouring
liquorice and assorted sweets, to decorate

1  Preheat the oven to 120°C (235°F/Gas 1/2). Grease two baking trays and line with baking paper.

2  Beat the egg whites in a bowl using electric beaters until soft peaks form.

3  Add the sugar gradually, beating until the mixture is thick and glossy, and the sugar has dissolved.

4  Divide the meringue mixture in half. Add a few drops of green food colouring to one bowl and a few drops of red to the other and beat.

5  Spoon each meringue mixture into a separate piping bag, fitted with a 1 cm (1/2 inch) plain, round nozzle.

6  Pipe caterpillar shapes about 8–10 cm (3 1/4–4 inch) long with the green meringue onto the trays. Pipe snail shapes with the pink meringue.

7  Decorate snails and caterpillars with assorted sweets to form features. Bake for 55–60 minutes, or until crisp. Turn off the oven but leave the meringues inside until completely cool.

# coconut clusters

**MAKES 30**

250 g (9 oz) desiccated coconut
200 g (7 oz) condensed milk
1 teaspoon vanilla extract
glacé cherries, to decorate

1  Preheat the oven to 180°C (350°F/Gas 4). Lightly grease two baking trays.

2  Combine the coconut, condensed milk and vanilla in a bowl.

3  Drop 1 teaspoonsful at a time onto the trays. Decorate the mounds with the cherries.

4  Bake for 10–12 minutes, or until lightly browned. Remove from trays and allow to cool.

# caramel centres

**MAKES 36**

300 g (10½ oz) unsalted butter

125 g (4½ oz/½ cup) caster (superfine) sugar

2 teaspoons vanilla extract

185 g (6½ oz/1½ cups) plain (all-purpose) flour

85 g (3 oz/⅔ cup) self-raising flour

**caramel topping**

50 g (1¾ oz) unsalted butter, cubed and softened

2 tablespoons soft brown sugar

1 tablespoon golden syrup

125 ml (4 fl oz/½ cup) condensed milk

100 g (3½ oz) chocolate, melted

1 Preheat the oven to 180°C (350°F/Gas 4). Line 2 baking trays with baking paper.

2 Beat the butter and sugar until creamy and add the vanilla. Stir in the combined sifted flours and mix to a smooth dough.

3 Roll 3 teaspoons of the mixture into balls and place on the trays. Using your thumb, make a deep indentation in the centre of each biscuit. Bake for 10–15 minutes, or until lightly golden. Leave for 5 minutes, then cool on a wire rack.

4 To make the caramel topping, place the butter, sugar and syrup in a heavy-based pan. Stir over low heat until the sugar dissolves. Add the condensed milk and stir for about 5–10 minutes, or until golden.

5 Fill the cavity of each biscuit with the caramel and cool. When the caramel is cold, flatten with a wet finger.

6 Spread the chocolate on top.

# alphabet cookies

## MAKES ABOUT 20

### vanilla cookies

125 g (4¹/₂ oz) unsalted butter, softened

125 g (4¹/₂ oz) caster (superfine) sugar

30 ml (1 fl oz) milk

1 teaspoon vanilla extract

185 g (6¹/₂ oz/1¹/₂ cups) self-raising flour

60 g (2¹/₄ oz/¹/₂ cup) custard powder

### icing (frosting)

60 g (2¹/₄ oz/¹/₂ cup) icing (confectioners') sugar, sifted

5 g (¹/₈ oz) butter

1 tablespoons hot water

¹/₄ teaspoon vanilla extract

few drops of various food colouring (optional)

1  Preheat the oven to 190°C (375°F/Gas 5). Line two trays with baking paper.

2  Beat the butter and caster sugar in a bowl using electric beaters for 3–5 minutes, or until fluffy.

3  Add the milk and vanilla extract and beat until combined. Add the self-raising flour and custard powder and use a knife to mix to a soft dough.

4  Turn onto a floured surface and knead for 1 minute, or until smooth. Roll out the dough between two sheets of baking paper, to 5 mm (¹/₄ inch) thick.

5  Cut the dough into shapes using alphabet cutters. Press the remaining dough together and re-roll. Cut out shapes and place the biscuits on the trays.

6  Bake for 15–18 minutes, until golden. Cool on the trays for 3 minutes, then transfer to a wire rack to cool.

7  To make the icing, blend all the ingredients together until smooth. If using various colours, separate into bowls, then add colouring. Spread over the biscuits.

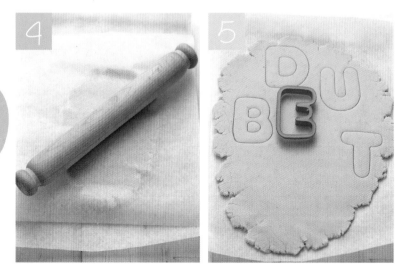

# monte creams

125 g (4$^1$/$_2$ oz) unsalted butter

115 g (4 oz/$^1$/$_2$ cup) caster (superfine) sugar

3 tablespoons milk

185 g (6$^1$/$_2$ oz/1$^1$/$_2$ cups) self-raising flour

30 g (1 oz/$^1$/$_4$ cup) custard powder

30 g (1 oz/$^1$/$_3$ cup) desiccated coconut

custard powder, extra

**filling**

75 g (2$^3$/$_4$ oz) unsalted butter, softened

85 g (3 oz/$^2$/$_3$ cup) icing (confectioners') sugar

2 teaspoons milk

105 g (3$^3$/$_4$ oz/$^1$/$_3$ cup) strawberry jam

1 Preheat the oven to 180°C (350°F/Gas 4). Line two baking trays with baking paper.

2 Cream the butter and sugar in a bowl using electric beaters until light and fluffy. Add the milk and beat until combined. Sift the flour and custard powder and add to the bowl with the coconut. Mix to form a soft dough.

3 Roll 2 teaspoons of the mixture into balls. Place on the trays and press with a fork. Dip the fork in the extra custard powder occasionally to prevent sticking.

4 Bake for 15–20 minutes, or until golden. Transfer to a wire rack to cool completely.

5 To make the filling, beat the butter and icing sugar in a bowl using electric beaters until creamy. Beat in the milk.

6 Spread one biscuit with $^1$/$_2$ teaspoon of the filling and one with $^1$/$_2$ teaspoon of jam, then press together.

# chocolate hazelnut friands

### MAKES 12

185 g (6¹/₂ oz) unsalted butter

6 egg whites

155 g (5¹/₂ oz/1¹/₄ cups) plain (all-purpose) flour

30 g (1 oz/¹/₄ cup) unsweetened cocoa powder

250 g (9 oz/2 cups) confectioners') sugar

200 g (7 oz) ground hazelnuts

1. Preheat the oven to 200°C (400°F/Gas 6). Grease twelve 125 ml (4 fl oz/¹/₂ cup) friand holes.

2. Place the butter in a small saucepan and melt over medium heat. Cook for 3–4 minutes, or until it turns a deep golden colour. Set aside to cool.

3. Lightly whisk the egg whites in a bowl until frothy. Sift the flour, cocoa powder and icing sugar into a large bowl. Stir in the ground hazelnuts.

4. Make a well in the centre. Add the egg whites and butter and mix until combined. Spoon the mixture into the friand holes until three-quarters filled.

5. Bake for 20–25 minutes, or until a skewer inserted into the centre comes out clean. Leave in the tin for a few minutes, then cool on a wire rack.

# madeleines

### MAKES 14
### (OR 30 SMALL ONES)

3 eggs

100 g (3¹/₂ oz/¹/₂ cup) caster (superfine) sugar

150 g (5¹/₂ oz/1¹/₄ cups) plain (all-purpose) flour

100 g (3¹/₂ oz) unsalted butter, melted

grated zest of 1 lemon and 1 orange

1. Preheat the oven to 200°C (400°F/Gas 6). Brush a tray of madeleine moulds with melted butter and coat with flour, then tap the tray to remove the excess flour.

2. Whisk the eggs and sugar until the mixture is thick and pale and the whisk leaves a trail when lifted.

3. Gently fold in the flour, then the melted butter and grated lemon and orange zest. Spoon into the moulds, leaving a little room for rising.

4. Bake for 12 minutes (small madeleines will only need 7 minutes), or until very lightly golden. Turn out onto a wire rack to cool.

# cakes and slices

# carrot cake with ricotta topping

### SERVES 12–14

310 g (11 oz/2¹/₂ cups) self-raising flour

1 teaspoon bicarbonate of soda (baking soda)

2 teaspoons ground cinnamon

1 teaspoon mixed (pumpkin pie) spice

90 g (3¹/₄ oz/¹/₂ cup) soft brown sugar

60 g (2¹/₄ oz/¹/₂ cup) sultanas (golden raisins)

2 eggs, lightly beaten

2 tablespoons canola oil

4 tablespoons milk

140 g (5 oz/¹/₂ cup) apple purée

300 g (10¹/₂ oz) carrots, coarsely grated

### ricotta topping

125 g (4¹/₂ oz/¹/₂ cup) ricotta cheese

30 g (1 oz/¹/₄ cup) icing (confectioners') sugar

1 teaspoon grated lime zest

1 Preheat the oven to 180°C (350°F/Gas 4). Lightly grease a 10 x 18 cm (4 x 7 inch) loaf (bar) tin and line the base with baking paper. Sift the flour, bicarbonate soda and spices into a large bowl. Stir in the brown sugar and sultanas.

2 Combine the eggs, oil, milk and apple purée. Stir the egg mixture into the flour mixture.

3 Add the carrot and mix well to combine. Spread into the tin and bake for 1 hour 15 minutes, or until the cake comes away slightly from the sides. Leave for 5 minutes, then turn out onto a wire rack.

4 To make the topping, beat the ricotta, icing sugar and lime zest together until smooth. Spread over the cooled cake.

# mini mango cakes with lime syrup

**MAKES 4**

425 g (15 oz) tinned mango slices in syrup, drained

90 g (3¼ oz) unsalted butter, softened

185 g (6½ oz/¾ cup) caster (superfine) sugar

2 eggs, lightly beaten

60 g (2¼ oz/½ cup) self-raising flour

2 tablespoons ground almonds

2 tablespoons coconut milk

2 tablespoons lime juice

1 Preheat the oven to 200°C (400°F/Gas 6). Grease four standard muffin holes and line with mango slices.

2 Beat the butter and 125 g (4 fl oz/½ cup) of the sugar in a bowl using electric beaters until creamy. Gradually add the egg, beating well after each addition. Fold in the sifted flour, then add the almonds and coconut milk. Spoon into the muffin holes.

3 Bake for 25 minutes, or until lightly golden. Once cool, pierce holes in each cake with a skewer.

4 To make the syrup, put the lime juice, the remaining sugar and 125 ml (4 fl oz/½ cup) of water in a small saucepan and stir over low heat until the sugar dissolves. Increase the heat and simmer for 10 minutes.

5 Drizzle the syrup over the top. Stand for 5 minutes to soak up the liquid. Turn out and serve.

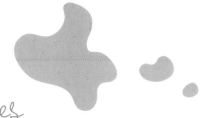

# raspberry and passionfruit cakes

### MAKES 6

30 g (1 oz/¼ cup) plain (all-purpose) flour

90 g (3¼ oz/¾ cup) self-raising flour

140 g (4⅔ oz/¾ cup) ground almonds

185 g (6½ oz) unsalted butter

250 g (9 oz/1 cup) caster (superfine) sugar

125 g (4½ oz/½ cup) fresh passionfruit pulp

2 teaspoons vanilla extract

2 eggs

125 g (4½ oz/1 cup) frozen or fresh raspberries

icing (confectioners') sugar, to dust

1 Preheat the oven to 180°C (350°F/Gas 4). Grease six 160 ml (5¼ fl oz) mini heart-shaped tins.

2 Combine the plain flour, self-raising flour and ground almonds in a large bowl. Make a well in the centre.

3 Put the butter, sugar, pulp and vanilla extract in a saucepan. Stir over low heat until the butter has melted and the mixture is smooth.

4 Whisk the butter mixture into the dry ingredients. Whisk in the eggs until smooth.

5 Pour the mixture into the tins. Drop the raspberries on top, pushing them just below the surface.

6 Bake for 25 minutes, or until lightly golden. Set aside for 10 minutes, then turn out onto a wire rack to cool. Dust with icing sugar to serve.

# lemon cake with crunchy topping

**SERVES 8–10**

250 g (9 oz) unsalted butter, softened

200 g (7 oz) caster (superfine) sugar

2 teaspoons finely grated lemon zest

4 eggs, lightly beaten

250 g (9 oz/2 cups) self-raising flour

1 teaspoon baking powder

2 tablespoons lemon juice

crunchy topping

110 g (3¾ oz/½ cup) sugar

3 tablespoons lemon juice

1 Preheat the oven to 170°C (325°F/Gas 3). Lightly grease a 22 cm (8½ inch) square cake tin. Line the base with baking paper.

2 Cream the butter and sugar in a bowl using electric beaters until light and fluffy. Add the lemon zest, then gradually add the egg, beating well after each addition.

3 Using a large metal spoon, fold in the combined sifted flour, baking powder and ¼ teaspoon salt, as well as the lemon juice. Stir until the mixture is just combined and almost smooth.

4 Spoon the mixture into the tin and smooth the surface. Bake for 1 hour 20 minutes, or until a skewer inserted into the centre of the cake comes out clean. Remove from the tin and turn out onto a wire rack.

5 To make the topping, mix together the sugar and lemon juice (do not dissolve the sugar), and quickly brush over the top of the warm cake. The juice will sink into the cake, and the sugar will form a crunchy topping. Allow to cool before serving.

# cherry ripple teacake

## SERVES 8–10

700 g (1 lb 9 oz) jar pitted cherries in syrup

1 tablespoon cornflour (cornstarch)

250 g (9 oz/2 cups) self-raising flour

165 g (5¾ oz/¾ cup) sugar

30 g (1 oz/⅓ cup) desiccated coconut

125 g (4½ oz) butter, chopped

1 egg

185 ml (6 fl oz/¾ cup) milk

1 Preheat oven to 180°C (350°F/Gas 4). Brush a 20 cm (8 inch) spring-form cake tin with melted butter. Line the base and sides with baking paper. Lightly grease the paper.

2 Drain the cherries, keeping 125 ml (4 fl oz/½ cup) of the syrup. Place the cherries in a saucepan. Blend the cornflour with the cherry syrup. Add to the saucepan. Stir over low heat until the mixture boils and thickens.

3 Sift the flour into a bowl. Add the sugar, coconut and butter. Rub the butter into the flour until it is crumbly. Measure out ½ cup of the mixture and set aside.

4 Add the egg and milk to the bowl and stir until almost smooth. Spoon the mixture into the tin and smooth the surface.

5 Spoon the cooled cherry mixture in small mounds over the top. Sprinkle over the ½ cup of coconut topping.

6 Bake for 50–55 minutes, or until lightly golden. Leave in the tin for 10 minutes, then turn out onto a wire rack to cool.

# sand cakes with passionfruit cream cheese icing

## MAKES 6

185 g (6½ oz) unsalted butter, softened

2 teaspoons vanilla extract

250 g (9 oz/1 cup) caster (superfine) sugar

3 eggs

185 g (6½ oz/1½ cups) self-raising flour

60 g (2¼ oz/⅓ cup) rice flour

4 tablespoons milk

### passionfruit cream cheese icing (frosting)

100 g (3⅓ oz) cream cheese, at room temperature

90 g (3¼ oz/¾ cup) icing (confectioners') sugar, sifted

1–2 tablespoons passionfruit pulp

1  Preheat the oven to 180°C (350°F/ Gas 4). Lightly grease six standard muffin holes and line the bases with baking paper.

2  Beat the butter, vanilla extract, sugar, eggs, flours and milk using electric beaters on low speed until combined, then beat on medium speed for 3 minutes, or until thick and creamy.

3  Pour the mixture into the prepared tin and smooth the surface.

4  Bake for 20–25 minutes, or lightly golden. Leave in the tin for 10 minutes, then turn out onto a wire rack to cool completely.

5  To make the icing, beat the cream cheese and icing sugar in a small bowl using electric beaters until light and creamy. Add the passionfruit pulp. Beat for 2 minutes, or until smooth and fluffy. Spoon over the cakes.

# fruity bran loaf

## MAKES 10–12 SLICES

60 g (2¼ oz/½ cup) chopped dried pears

60 g (2¼ oz/½ cup) chopped dried peaches

125 g (4½ oz/1 cup) dried fruit medley or chopped dried apricots

70 g (2½ oz/1 cup) processed wheat bran cereal

100 g (3½ oz/½ cup) soft brown sugar

375 ml (13 fl oz/1½ cups) reduced-fat milk

185 g (6½ oz/1¼ cups) stoneground self-raising flour

1 teaspoon mixed (pumpkin pie) spice

1 Put the pears, peaches, fruit medley, wheat bran cereal, brown sugar and milk in a large bowl. Stir to combine and set aside for 1 hour until the bran has softened.

2 Preheat the oven to 180°C (350°F/ Gas 4). Spray a 9.5 x 19.5 cm (3¾ x 7½ inch) loaf (bar) tin with oil, then line the base with baking paper.

3 Sift the flour and mixed spice into a bowl, then return any husks to the bowl. Stir into the fruit mixture. Spoon the mixture into the prepared tin and smooth the surface.

4 Bake for 45–50 minutes, or until lightly browned. Leave in the tin for 10 minutes, then turn out onto a wire rack to cool completely.

**Note:** This loaf will keep refrigerated for up to 1 week and frozen for up to 1 month.

# wholemeal apricot rock cakes

**MAKES 20**

225 g (8 oz/1½ cups) stoneground wholemeal self-raising flour

½ teaspoons baking powder

1½ teaspoons ground cinnamon

55 g (2 oz/½ cup) ground almonds

80 g (2¾ oz/⅓ cup) raw sugar

185 g (6½ oz/1 cup) dried apricots, chopped

1 tablespoon sunflower or pepitas (pumpkin seeds)

90 g (3¼ oz) butter, melted

1 egg, lightly beaten

3 tablespoons buttermilk

1  Preheat the oven to 180°C (350°F/Gas 4). Line a large baking tray with baking paper.

2  Sift the flour, baking powder and cinnamon into a large bowl, then return any husks to the bowl. Stir in the ground almonds, raw sugar, apricots and seeds. Make a well in the centre.

3  Combine the butter, egg and buttermilk in a small bowl. Pour into the well in the dry ingredients and mix briefly with a fork until just combined.

4  Using 1 heaped tablespoon of batter at a time, put spoonfuls onto the tray, forming a little mound.

5  Bake for 15–20 minutes, or until cooked. Leave on the tray for 2–3 minutes, then transfer to a wire rack to cool completely.

# pineapple upside-down cake

## SERVES 8–10

**base**

60 g (2¼ oz) unsalted butter

95 g (3¼ oz/½ cup) brown sugar

4 slices canned pineapple, drained and halved

12 glace cherries

**cake**

125 g (4½ oz) butter

115 g (4 oz/½ cup) caster (superfine) sugar

2 eggs

1 teaspoon vanilla extract

185 g (6½ oz/1½ cups) self raising flour, sifted

125 ml (4 fl oz/½ cup) milk

1. To prepare the base, cream the butter and sugar in a small bowl. Spread over the base of a 20 cm (8 inch) spring-form cake tin lined with baking paper.

2. Arrange the pineapple and cherries over base. Set aside.

3. To prepare the cake, preheat the oven to 180°C (350°F/Gas 4). Cream the butter and sugar until fluffy. Add the eggs one at a time, beating well after each addition. Stir in the vanilla extract.

4. Fold the flour into the creamed mixture alternately with milk, beginning and ending with flour.

5. Spread the cake mixture carefully over the base. Bake about 45–50 minutes. Cool in tin for 15 minutes, then turn out onto wire rack to cool completely.

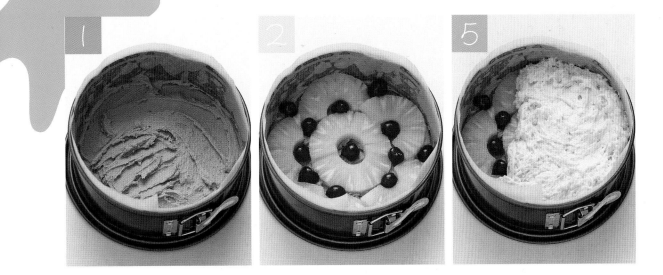

# yoghurt banana cakes with honey icing

**MAKES 6**

180 g (6 oz) unsalted butter, softened

90 g (3¹/₄ oz/¹/₄ cup) honey

230 g (8 oz/1 cup) caster (superfine) sugar

1¹/₂ teaspoons vanilla extract

3 eggs

360 g (12³/₄ oz/1¹/₂ cups) mashed ripe banana (about 4 bananas)

185 g (6¹/₂ oz/³/₄ cup) plain yoghurt

¹/₂ teaspoon bicarbonate of soda (baking soda)

375 g (13 oz/3 cups) self-raising flour, sifted

**honey icing (frosting)**

125 g (4¹/₂ oz) unsalted butter

3 tablespoons honey

125 g (4¹/₂ oz/1 cup) icing (confectioners') sugar

1 tablespoon milk

1 Preheat the oven to 180°C (350°F/Gas 4). Lightly grease six 10 cm (4 inch) round cake tins and line the bases with baking paper.

2 Cream the butter, honey, sugar and vanilla in a bowl using electric beaters until fluffy. Add the eggs one at a time, beating well after each addition, then beat in the banana.

3 Combine the yoghurt and bicarbonate of soda in a small bowl. Fold the flour alternately with the yoghurt into the banana mixture. Divide the mixture evenly between the tins, smoothing the tops.

4 Bake for 50–60 minutes, or until a skewer inserted into the centre of a cake comes out clean. Cool in the tins for 5 minutes, then turn out onto a wire rack.

5 To make the honey icing, cream the butter and honey in a small bowl using electric beaters until fluffy. Gradually add the icing sugar alternately with the milk, beating well until the mixture is very pale. When the cakes are cold, divide the honey icing between the tops, spreading the icing to form rough peaks.

**Note:** These cakes will keep, stored in an airtight container, for up to 4 days. Un-iced cakes can be frozen for up to 3 months.

# chocolate cake

**SERVES 8–10**

125 g (4½ oz) unsalted butter

170 g (6 oz/¾ cup) caster (superfine) sugar

3 eggs

1 tablespoon golden syrup or honey

1 teaspoon vanilla extract

185 g (6½ oz/1½ cups) plain (all-purpose) flour

½ teaspoon baking powder

¼ tablespoon bicarbonate of soda (baking soda)

3 tablespoons unsweetened cocoa powder

125 ml (4 fl oz/½ cup) milk

**icing**

125 g (4½ oz/1 cup) icing (confectioners') sugar

1½ tablespoons unsweetened cocoa powder

20 g (¾ oz) unsalted butter, softened

1  Preheat the oven to 180°C (350°F/Gas 4). Grease a 20 cm (8 inch) spring-form cake tin. Line with baking paper. Beat the butter, sugar and eggs until smooth and creamy.

2  Stir in the golden syrup and vanilla. Sift in the flour, baking powder, bicarbonate of soda and cocoa. Mix in the milk.

3  Spread evenly in the tin. Bake for 45–55 minutes.

4  Leave to stand for 10 minutes, then take out of the tin. Cool completely.

5  To make the icing, mix the icing sugar, cocoa and butter with a litle hot water. When smooth, spread over the cake.

# baked cheesecake

## SERVES 8–10

375 g (13 oz) plain sweet biscuits (cookies)

175 g (6 oz) unsalted butter, melted

### filling

500 g (1 lb 2 oz) cream cheese

200 g (7 oz) caster (superfine) sugar

4 eggs

300 ml (10½ fl oz) thick (double/heavy) cream

2 tablespoons plain (all-purpose) flour

1 teaspoon ground cinnamon

¼ teaspoon ground nutmeg

1 tablespoon lemon juice

2 teaspoons vanilla extract

1 Lightly grease a 23 cm (9 inch) round spring-form cake tin and line the base and side with baking paper.

2 Put the biscuits in a food processor and process into crumbs. Add the butter and process until well combined. Press firmly into the base and side of the tin. Refrigerate for 1 hour. Preheat the oven to 180°C (350°F/Gas 4).

3 To make the filling, beat the cream cheese and sugar together until creamy. Add the eggs and cream and beat for about 4 minute. Fold in the flour, cinnamon, nutmeg, lemon juice and vanilla.

4 Pour the filling into the chilled crust and smooth the surface. Bake for 1 hour, or until golden. Allow to cool to room temperature, then refrigerate until ready to serve.

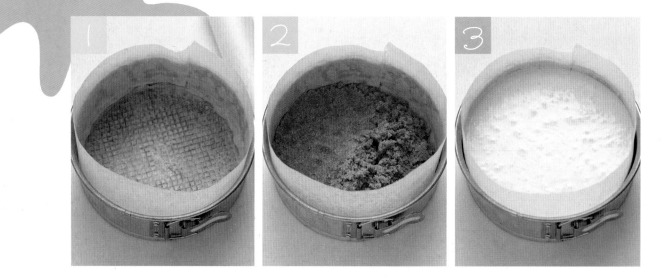

# lemon coconut cakes

**MAKES 5**

185 g (6¹/₂ oz/1¹/₂ cups) self-raising flour

45 g (1³/₄ oz/¹/₂ cup) desiccated coconut

1 tablespoon grated lemon zest

230 g (8¹/₂ oz/1 cup) caster (superfine) sugar

125 g (4¹/₂ oz) unsalted butter, melted

2 eggs

250 ml (9 fl oz/1 cup) milk

**coconut icing (frosting)**

185 g (6¹/₂ oz/1¹/₂ cups) icing (confectioners') sugar, sifted

90 g (3¹/₄ oz/1 cup) desiccated coconut, plus extra, to decorate

¹/₂ teaspoon grated lemon zest

3 tablespoons lemon juice

1 Preheat the oven to 180°C (350°F/Gas 4). Lightly grease five 175 ml (5¹/₂ fl oz) mini bundt tins.

2 Sift the flour into a large bowl and add the coconut, lemon zest, sugar, butter, eggs and milk. Mix well with a wooden spoon until smooth. Pour into the tins and smooth the surface.

3 Bake for 20–25 minutes, or until lightly golden. Leave the cakes in the tins for 5 minutes, then turn out onto a wire rack to cool completely.

4 To make the icing, combine the icing sugar and coconut in a bowl. Add the lemon zest and lemon juice.

5 Top the cakes with the icing and decorate with the extra coconut.

# cinnamon teacake

## SERVES 8

60 g (2¼ oz) butter

115 g (4 oz/½ cup) caster (superfine) sugar

1 egg, lightly beaten

1 teaspoon vanilla extract

90 g (3¼ oz/¾ cup) self-raising flour

30 g (1 oz/¼ cup) plain (all-purpose) flour

1 teaspoon ground cinnamon

125 ml (4 fl oz/½ cup) milk

### topping

1 tablespoon caster (superfine) sugar

1 teaspoon ground cinnamon

20 g (¾ oz) butter, melted

1 Preheat the oven to 180°C (350°F/Gas 4). Lightly grease a 20 cm (8 inch) round cake tin. Line the base with baking paper.

2 Beat the butter and sugar using electric beaters until light and creamy. Add the beaten egg gradually, beating well after each addition. Add the vanilla extract and beat until combined.

3 Transfer the mixture to a large bowl. Using a spoon, fold in the sifted flours and cinnamon alternately with the milk. Stir until smooth.

4 Spoon into the tin and smooth the surface. Bake for 35–40 minutes, or until a skewer comes out clean when inserted into the centre. Leave the cake in the tin for 5 minutes, then turn out onto a wire rack.

5 Combine the sugar and cinnamon. Brush the cake with the melted butter while still warm. Sprinkle the cake with the sugar and cinnamon.

# upside-down banana cake

**SERVES 6**

125 g (4½ oz) unsalted butter

185 g (6½ oz/¾ cup) caster (superfine) sugar

1 egg

250 g (9 oz/2 cups) plain (all-purpose) flour

2 teaspoons baking powder

185 ml (6 fl oz/¾ cup) milk

1 large banana, mashed

75 g (2½ oz) unsalted butter, melted

95 g (3¼ oz/½ cup) soft brown sugar

260 g (9¼ oz/1 cup) tinned crushed pineapple, drained

cream, to serve

1. Preheat the oven to 180°C (350°F/Gas 4). Grease six small spring-form cake tins or a 20 cm (8 inch) spring-form cake tin.

2. Beat the butter, sugar and egg until smooth. Sift in the flour and baking powder. Mix well, then add the milk and mashed banana.

3. Spread the melted butter in the base of each tin, then sprinkle evenly with the brown sugar.

4. Spread the crushed pineapple over the sugar. Pour the batter evenly over the top. Bake for 40–45 minutes.

5. Tip out onto a plate. Serve warm with cream.

# coconut jam slice

## MAKES 20

125 g (4½ oz/1 cup) plain (all-purpose) flour

60 g (2¼ oz/½ cup) self-raising flour

150 g (5½ oz) unsalted butter, cubed

60 g (2¼ oz/½ cup) icing (confectioners') sugar

1 egg yolk

160 g (5¾ oz/½ cup) strawberry jam

125 g (4½ oz) caster (superfine) sugar

3 eggs

270 g (9½ oz/3 cups) desiccated coconut

1 Preheat the oven to 180°C (350°F/Gas 4). Lightly grease a shallow 23 cm (9 inch) square tin and line with baking paper, leaving the paper hanging over on two opposite sides.

2 Put the flour and icing sugar in a bowl and rub in the butter with your fingertips until the mixture is crumbly. Mix in the egg yolk and gather together.

3 Press the dough into the tin and refrigerate for 10 minutes. Bake for 15 minutes, or until golden brown. Allow to cool, then spread the jam evenly over the pastry.

4 Beat the caster sugar and eggs together until creamy, then stir in the coconut. Spread the mixture over the jam, gently pressing down with the back of a spoon.

5 Bake for 25–30 minutes, or until lightly golden. Leave to cool in the tin, then lift the slice out, using the paper as handles. Cut the slice into pieces.

**Note:** Store in an airtight container for up to 4 days.

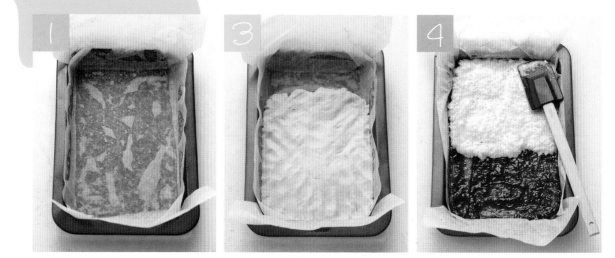

# caramel slice

## MAKES 18–20 SLICES

60 g (2¼ oz/½ cup) plain (all-purpose) flour

60 g (2¼ oz/½ cup) self-raising flour

90 g (3¼ oz/1 cup) desiccated coconut

100 g (3½ oz) unsalted butter

115 g (4 oz/½ cup) soft brown sugar

### filling

30 g (1 oz) unsalted butter

2 tablespoons golden syrup or honey

400 g (14 oz) sweetened condensed milk

### topping

150 g (5½ oz) dark chocolate, roughly chopped

40 g (1½ oz) unsalted butter

1 Preheat the oven to 180°C (350°F/Gas 4). Line a shallow 28 x 18 cm (11¼ x 7 inch) baking tin. Sift the flours together into a bowl. Stir in the coconut and make a well in the centre.

2 Combine the butter and sugar in a saucepan and stir over low heat until the butter has melted. Pour into the dry ingredients and stir well to combine.

3 Press the mixture evenly into the tin with the back of a spoon. Bake for 10 minutes, then leave to cool.

4 To make the filling, combine the butter, syrup and condensed milk in a saucepan. Stir over low heat until smooth. Continue stirring for 10 minutes. Pour over the pastry base and bake for 20 minutes.

5 To make the topping, place the chocolate and butter in a heatproof bowl over a saucepan of barely simmering water. Stir until smooth.

6 Spread over the caramel and leave to set. Lift the slice from the tin and cut into bars or squares to serve.

# swiss roll

## SERVES 10

90 g (3¼ oz/¾ cup) self-raising flour

3 eggs, lightly beaten

170 g (6 oz/¾ cup) caster (superfine) sugar

160 g (5¾ oz/½ cup) strawberry jam, beaten

icing (confectioners') sugar, to dust

1 Preheat the oven to 190°C (375°F/Gas 5). Lightly grease a shallow 2 x 25 x 30 cm (¾ x 10 x 12 inch) Swiss roll tin (jelly roll tin). Line the base with baking paper, extending over the two long sides. Sift the flour three times onto baking paper.

2 Beat the eggs in a bowl using electric beaters for 5 minutes, or until thick and pale. Add 115 g (4 oz/ ½ cup) of the sugar gradually, beating until the mixture is pale. Transfer to a large bowl.

3 Using a metal spoon, fold in the flour quickly. Spread into the tin and smooth the surface.

4 Bake for 10–12 minutes, or until lightly golden and springy to the touch. Leave in the tin.

5 Place a tea towel on the kitchen bench. Cover with baking paper and sprinkle with the remaining caster sugar. Turn the cake out onto the baking paper.

6 Roll the cake up from the short side, rolling the paper inside the roll. Put the rolled cake on a wire rack for 5 minutes, then unroll and allow the cake to cool.

7 Spread with the jam and re-roll. Trim the ends with a knife. Sprinkle with icing sugar.

# rhubarb and apple crumble slice

**MAKES 12 PIECES**

310 g (11 oz/2½ cups) plain (all-purpose) flour

270 g (9½ oz) unsalted butter, softened

80 g (2¾ oz) caster (superfine) sugar

1 egg yolk

200 g (7 oz) slivered almonds

400 g (14 oz) tinned pie apple

500 g (1 lb 2 oz) rhubarb, drained

1 teaspoon grated lemon zest

icing (confectioners') sugar, to dust

1  Preheat the oven to 180°C (350°F/Gas 4). Lightly grease a 20 x 30 cm (8 x 12 inch) baking tin. Lline with baking paper, hanging over the two long sides.

2  Put 185 g (6½ oz) of flour, 145 g (5 oz) butter and 25 g (1 oz) caster sugar in a food processor and mix in short bursts until the mixture resembles fine crumbs. Add the egg yolk and 2 tablespoons cold water and mix in short bursts to combine.

3  Press into the tin and bake for 15 minutes. Allow to cool.

4  Place the remaining flour, butter, and sugar in the food processor with 150 g (5½ oz) of the almonds and mix in short bursts until the almonds are chopped. Set aside 1 cup of mixture.

5  Fold the remaining crumb mixture, apple, rhubarb and lemon zest together.

6  Cover the base of the tin with the fruit. Sprinkle with the reserved crumble, then with the remaining slivered almonds.

7  Bake for 40 minutes. Leave in the tin for 5 minutes, then turn out onto a wire rack to cool. Cut into slices and dusting with icing sugar.

# chocolate cheese swirls

## MAKES 24 PIECES

1.25 kg (2 lb 12 oz) cream cheese, at room temperature

120 g (4¼ oz) ricotta cheese

3 teaspoons vanilla extract

310 g (11 oz/1¼ cups) caster (superfine) sugar

6 eggs

100 g (3½ oz) dark chocolate, broken into pieces

1 tablespoon milk

2 teaspoons powdered drinking chocolate

75 g (2½ oz) ground hazelnuts

3 teaspoons grated orange zest

50 g (1¾ oz) crushed amaretti biscuits

icing (confectioners') sugar, to dust

1   Preheat the oven to 170°C (325°F/Gas 3). Lightly grease a 20 x 30 cm (8 x 12 inch) shallow baking tin. Line with baking paper, extending over the two long sides.

2   Blend the cream cheese, ricotta, vanilla and sugar in a food processor until smooth. Add the eggs and process until smooth. Divide the mixture between two bowls.

3   Bring a saucepan of water to the boil and remove from the heat. Put the chocolate, milk and drinking chocolate in a heatproof bowl and place over the water. Make the bowl doesn't touch the water. Stir occasionally until melted. Cool.

4   Add to one of the bowls of cream cheese. Mix well, then stir in the hazelnuts. Pour into the tin.

5   Stir the orange zest and biscuits into the other bowl of cream cheese. Mix well, then gently spoon over the chocolate mix, covering it completely.

6   With a knife and starting in one corner, cut the orange mix down through the chocolate, bringing the chocolate up in swirls through the orange.

7   Bake for 1 hour, or until set. Cool in the tin. Lift out and cut into squares. Dust with icing sugar to serve.

# two-tone fudge brownies

## MAKES 20

125 g (4¹/2 oz) unsalted butter

90 g (3¹/4 oz) chopped milk chocolate

250 g (9 oz) sugar

2 teaspoons vanilla extract

2 eggs

120 g (4¹/4 oz) sifted plain (all-purpose) flour

90 g (3¹/4 oz) white chocolate buttons

1 Preheat the oven to 180°C (350°F/Gas 4). Grease a 20 cm (8 inch) square cake tin.

2 Stir 60 g (2¹/4 oz) of the butter and the chopped milk chocolate in a heatproof bowl set over a saucepan of simmering water until just melted.

3 Beat 125 g (4¹/2 oz) sugar, 1 teaspoon vanilla extract and 1 egg in a bowl and stir in the chocolate mixture. Stir in 60 g (2¹/4 oz) of the plain flour until combined, then set aside.

4 Stir 60 g (2¹/4 oz) of the butter and the white chocolate buttons in a heatproof bowl set over a saucepan of simmering water until just melted.

5 Beat 125 g (4¹/2 oz) sugar, 1 teaspoon vanilla extract and 1 egg in a bowl and stir in the white chocolate mixture. Stir in 60 g (2¹/4 oz) of the plain flour until combined, then set aside.

6 Drop large spoonfuls of the two mixtures into the tin, without mixing them together. Gently smooth the surface and bake for 35 minutes, or until firm. Cool in the tin before cutting.

desserts and
party treats

# raspberry shortcake

## SERVES 6

### pastry

125 g (4½ oz/1 cup) plain (all-purpose) flour

40 g (1½ oz/⅓ cup) icing (confectioners') sugar

90 g (3¼ oz) unsalted butter, chilled and chopped

1 egg yolk

½ teaspoon natural vanilla extract

½–1 tablespoon iced water

### topping

750 g (1 lb 10 oz/6 cups) fresh raspberries

30 g (1 oz/¼ cup) icing (confectioners') sugar

110 g (3¾ oz/⅓ cup) redcurrant jelly

whipped cream, to serve

1 To make the pastry, sift the flour and icing sugar into a large bowl. Using your fingertips, rub in the butter until the mixture resembles fine breadcrumbs. Add the egg yolk, vanilla extract and enough of the iced water to make the ingredients come together, then mix to a dough with a flat-bladed knife, using a cutting action. Turn out onto a lightly floured work surface and gather together into a ball. Flatten slightly, wrap in plastic wrap and then refrigerate for 30 minutes.

2 Preheat oven to 180°C (350°F/Gas 4). Roll out the pastry to fit six small 5 x 10 cm (2 x 4 inch) fluted loose-based flan (tart) tins and trim the edge. Prick all over with a fork and refrigerate for 20 minutes.

3 Line the pastry with baking paper and spread a layer of baking beads or uncooked rice evenly over the paper. Bake for 15–20 minutes, or until golden. Remove the paper and beads and then bake for another 15 minutes. Cool on a wire rack.

4 To make the topping, set aside 500 g (1 lb 2 oz/ 4 cups) raspberries and mash the rest with the icing sugar. Spread the mashed raspberries over the shortcake just before serving.

5 Cover with the whole raspberries. Heat the redcurrant jelly in a small saucepan until melted and smooth. Use a soft pastry brush to coat the raspberries heavily with the warm redcurrant glaze. Cut into slices and serve with cream.

# fresh fruit tarts

### MAKES 36

750 g (1 lb 10 oz) ready-made sweet shortcrust pastry

**kiwi fruit tarts**

250 g (9 oz) cream cheese, at room temperature

4 tablespoons icing (confectioners') sugar

1 teaspoon grated lemon zest

1 teaspoon lemon juice

1–2 kiwi fruit, sliced, to serve

110 g (3¾ oz) apple baby gel

**blueberry tarts**

2 tablespoons cornflour (cornstarch)

1 teaspoon grated lemon zest

2 tablespoons lemon juice

2 tablespoons caster (superfine) sugar

185 ml (6 fl oz/¾ cup) milk

1 egg, lightly beaten

3 tablespoons pouring (whipping) cream

250 g (9 oz) fresh blueberries

icing (confectioners') sugar, to dust

1 Roll out the pastry and cut out 12 rounds using a 7 cm (2¾ inch) cutter. Line deep patty pans with the pastry rounds. Refrigerate for 10 minutes.

2 Cover each pastry shell with baking paper and fill with baking beads. Bake for 10 minutes. Remove from the oven and remove the baking paper and beads. Bake the pastry for a further 5–7 minutes, or until lightly golden. Cool before filling.

3 To make the kiwi fruit tarts, beat the cream cheese, icing sugar, lemon zest and juice using electric beaters. Spoon into the pastry cases. Arrange slices of kiwi fruit over the cream. Gently heat the apple gel until melted, then brush over the fruit.

4 To make the blueberry tarts, combine the cornflour, lemon zest, juice, caster sugar, milk and egg in a saucepan. Stir over low heat until the mixture boils and thickens, then cook for 1 minute. Cover and cool to room temperature, then whisk in the cream. Spoon into the pastry cases and cover with the blueberries. Sprinkle with icing sugar.

# bread and butter pudding

## SERVES 4

butter, for greasing

6 slices bread

750 ml (26 fl oz/3 cups) milk

1/4 teaspoon lemon zest

110 g (3³/4 oz/1/2 cup) sugar

4 eggs

125 g (4¹/2 oz/²/3 cup) dried mixed fruits (sultanas/golden raisins, raisins, chopped dried apricots, currants, mixed peel/mixed candied citrus peel)

1 Preheat the oven to 180°C (350°F/Gas 4). Grease a large ovenproof dish or four small dishes. Butter the bread and cut off the crusts.

2 Heat the milk in a saucepan and add the lemon zest. Bring to the boil, then cover and remove from the heat, leaving the milk to infuse for 10 minutes. Beat the sugar and eggs together, then strain the milk over the eggs and mix well.

3 Scatter half the dried fruit over the bottom of the dish and arrange half the bread, buttered sides down, on top. Pour in half the custard, then repeat with the remaining fruit, bread and custard.

4 Put the ovenproof dish or dishes in a large roasting tin. Pour water into the tin to come halfway up the side of the dish (this is called a bain-marie). Bake for 35 minutes.

# sticky date pudding

### SERVES 6

45 g (1½ oz/½ cup) desiccated coconut

115 g (4 oz/½ cup) soft brown sugar

90 g (3¼ oz/¾ cup) self-raising flour

30 g (1 oz/¼ cup) plain (all-purpose) flour

½ teaspoon bicarbonate of soda (baking soda)

100 g (3½ oz) unsalted butter

90 g (3 oz/¼ cup) golden syrup or honey

185 g (6½ oz/1 cup) chopped dates

3 tablespoons orange juice

2 eggs, lightly beaten

#### sauce

80 g (2¾ oz) unsalted butter

55 g (2 oz/¼ cup) soft brown sugar

250 ml (9 fl oz/1 cup) cream

2 tablespoons golden syrup or honey

1. Preheat the oven to 180°C (350°F/Gas 4). Brush six small pudding bowls with melted butter or oil.

2. Combine 2 tablespoons each of the coconut and brown sugar and sprinkle into the bowls.

3. Sift the flours and soda into a mixing bowl. Add the remaining coconut and make a well in the centre.

4. Combine the remaining sugar, butter, golden syrup, dates and orange juice in a saucepan. Stir over medium heat until the butter melts.

5. Using a metal spoon, fold the date mixture into the dry ingredients. Add the eggs and stir until smooth.

6. Pour the mixture into the bowls and bake for 35 minutes. Leave the puddings in the bowls for 5 minutes before turning out.

7. To make the sauce, combine all the ingredients in a saucepan. Stir over low heat until the sugar and butter have dissolved. Stir for a further 2 minutes, then serve over the hot pudding.

# caramel scrolls

## MAKES 16

310 g (11 oz/2½ cups) self-raising flour

115 g (4 oz/½ cup) caster (superfine) sugar

125 g (4½ oz) butter

125 ml (4 fl oz/½ cup) milk

3 tablespoons sour cream

60 g (2¼ oz) butter, extra, softened

60 g (2¼ oz/⅓ cup) soft brown sugar

### caramel icing (frosting)

45 g (1½ oz) butter

45 g (1½ oz/¼ cup) soft brown sugar

1 tablespoon milk

60 g (2¼ oz/½ cup) icing (confectioners') sugar, sifted

1 Preheat the oven to 210°C (415°F/Gas 6–7). Brush a shallow 23 cm (9 inch) square cake tin with oil.

2 Sift the flour into a bowl. Add the caster sugar and butter. Rub the butter into the flour until crumbly.

3 Add the combined milk and sour cream to the bowl. Stir until the mixture is almost smooth.

4 Turn the dough onto a floured surface. Knead until smooth. Roll out the dough on a floured surface to a large rectangle.

5 Combine the extra butter and brown sugar in a bowl. Spread the mixture evenly over the dough.

6 Roll dough from the long side into a log. Cut into 16 pieces. Place the slices, flat side down, in the tin.

7 Bake for 25 minutes, or until lightly golden.

8 To make the icing, melt the butter in a saucepan. Add the brown sugar and milk. Stir over low heat for 1 minute. Add the icing sugar and stir until smooth. Spread the cakes with the icing.

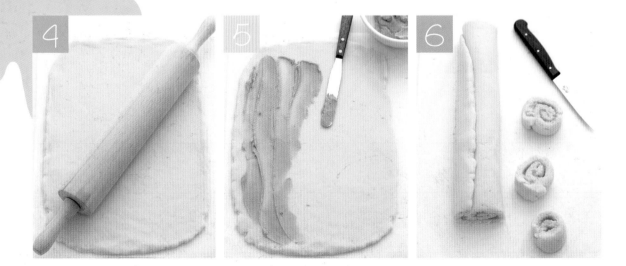